BLEMISHED
BUT NOT BROKEN

*May your light always
shine bright ♡
K Kinsley Adams*

KAY KINSLEY ADAMS

BALBOA.
PRESS

A DIVISION OF HAY HOUSE

Balboa Press books may be ordered through booksellers or by contacting:

Balboa Press
A Division of Hay House
1663 Liberty Drive
Bloomington, IN 47403
www.balboapress.com
1 (877) 407-4847

Print information available on the last page.

ISBN: 978-1-5043-7404- 0 (sc)
ISBN: 978-1-5043-7406-4 (hc)
ISBN: 978-1-5043-7405-7 (e)

Library of Congress Control Number: 2017901459

Balboa Press rev. date: 02/02/2017

Dedication

To my loving and wonderful husband who patiently observed my struggles with the computer over the course of writing this manuscript; to my mother, brothers and sister, and to my father who is keeping watch over all of us from above; and to my forever friend, Danielle.

Acknowledgement

Thanks to Jennifer Collins for the editing of my manuscript, and for patiently working with me as I was healing, as well as for her kindness and understanding, and providing me with wonderful perspective. It's been a real pleasure to get to know and work with her.

Thanks also to Zahid Hosssain for his wisdom and for the encouragement to share my story through the writing of this book.

Preface

Relationships can be complicated, and even more so if someone who you love struggles with an illness that is difficult to physically see. Growing up with a mother who has a mental illness was very challenging, but while I didn't know it as a child, there are tons of other families facing such difficulties. Sometimes it's far too easy to feel alone, as I often felt that my family was different and that I was, as well. I wrote this book with the hope that my story will help someone else to know that they are not all alone.

For many years, I attempted to write down my feelings about my life and the events as they were unrolling. My attempts to write my story would end up being crumpled into a ball and thrown into the wastepaper can. It was hard to describe what I was feeling, though, and sometimes the realization of what I'd just written was just too much to deal with. I sometimes even wondered who would believe such a story.

In November of 2015, though, I was re-inspired to write my story. At the time, I was dissatisfied with my work and the environment in which I was employed, and I knew that there was something else I was designed to do. As a result of questioning my path in life, I started to do some deep soul searching. Pushing me forward was the fact that I'd grown up with a strong father who inspired good morals and religious participation as a protestant. The belief in a loving God has been a strong guiding force, as I have sometimes struggled to keep the darkness out and the light in. Along with my religious upbringing, I've always had a deep sense of spirituality, and consistently been seeking answers about the great unknown.

In my search for answers about my life and the path I was to be on, I went with a friend to a local mystic fair. It was at this fair that I met a local astrologist and palmist who was filled with wisdom... I still recall his laugh when I told him what I did for a living. I was in sales and marketing at the time, though truth be told, my real role was a far cry from sales and marketing since I served as the department for complaints more than anything. I despised going to my office because it was filled with negative people who were also unhappy with their jobs. His laugh regarding my position took me by surprise, though, as it seemed that he immediately understood what I was going through.

As he looked at my palm and my astrological chart – based on my personal data of matters such as time and birthplace – he proceeded to tell me that I had not fulfilled my life calling. I looked at him with anticipation as he continued to tell me that I was meant to be writing my book. He told me that I had a story to tell, and that it was meant to be told in order to help other people. Being the wise man that he was, he also shared with me that writing my story would be a healing process for myself, and would take me to new heights. He shared that I could write my story or not, and that we all have free will to make our decisions, but he also proceeded to tell me why I'd been unable to write it in the past, and what I needed to do in order to best express myself.

The palmist also saw a blemish on the palm of my hand and asked me about it, and how long it had been there. It was the first time that I'd really taken notice of it, as it was rather small and I had not noticed it previously. That was all that he said about it, though, and I thought it was a strange inquiry... as the size of the blemish was small, though it was brown in color. Several months later, his comment about my blemish would bring about the name of my book.

Through that conversation, I felt inspired, and I had the belief that I could tell my story. Two months later, I lost my job as a result of speaking out about an injustice in the workplace, and suddenly I had the time and the inclination to write... so for three months, that is all that I did. And I cried and I laughed as I thought about my life and all of the characters I have encountered. It was very healing, as I worked my way through my past wounds.

My wounds inspired the cover of my book as I sat at my desk writing one afternoon. On top of my desk sat a stone heart that I had collected somewhere along the way. I took it in my hand and looked at all of the scars and markings, and then glimpsed the blemish on my hand. I thought of myself like the heart, as it was blemished but not broken and was still in one piece. With the heart in my hand, I stood up and went across the room to a painting that my husband had painted while he was in art school many moons ago. It's a collage of color on a canvas that is full of life. My instincts led me to go over and give it a closer look, and I took the canvas down and placed the blemished heart on top of it... and so the cover of this book was born.

Not only was my cover born, but a new marital relationship was also born. Until the writing of this book, I had not revealed my entire story to my husband. He underwent quite a learning experience about the woman who he had married! He was very understanding, though, as he hadn't before known about some of the romantic relationships that I had been involved in, or the depth of the wounds that I carried because I had always covered them up. It is a relief to me not to have to hide who I really am anymore. I don't carry the shame that I once did, and I now realize that everyone has something that they would rather not have anyone know about.

I have used a pen name and I have changed the names of the people who I love, but this is a true story, and not knowing exact identities does not change the facts of my journey. My intention is not to hurt anyone, as I love my family and friends. At the time of this writing, my mother is still living and, as for some of the other characters... well, I have lost touch with a few of them. More than anything, though, I hope that my writing my story will benefit someone else in some way – even if it is simply to let them know that they are not alone.

May your light always shine bright!

Kay

New Jersey – 1981

I was laying on the beach at the Jersey shore in the summer of 1981. I had just graduated from college in January, and had arrived a few days earlier to search for a job. Taking a break on that particularly warm day in early June, I was in a relaxed state of mind – despite the confusion from the past that I had left behind. I could hear the waves hitting the sand with a thundering roar as they rolled back and forth against the beach. The seagulls were crying overhead as they searched for any leftovers that might be available for a grab-and-go lunch, and I was laying comfortably on my colorful beach towel, even appreciating the feel of the grains of sand that had attached themselves to my feet. I could feel the warmth of the sun, and it felt nice against my sun-starved flesh. I loved to bathe in the sun, and I was in my glory. As I lay there in a trance-like state with my eyes shut to shield them against the glaring sun, I was simply enjoying the noises around me... when I recalled a horrible childhood memory. The memory came flooding in as though the sound of the waves had forced its appearance. The images were so impactful and full of surprise that it took me a few moments to truly realize that it was not a dream, and that I was recalling something that had actually happened to me.

I remembered that I'd been approximately five or six years old at the time, and that I'd been with my sister May. May was almost like a twin in the fact that we'd been born only eleven months apart. Growing up, we did everything together and we were inseparable. In the memory, May was standing with me at the entrance of an old chicken coop that had been converted into a playhouse for my older brother William and his friends. They sometimes even spent the night in that stinky old coop which sat on the northern edge of our property. This particular day, William was inside the coop with his friend, Brady. Brady was our next-door neighbor, and he had two sisters who were close in age and who we sometimes played with in our small backyard. We had spent that summer having fun and splashing around in our small wading pool.

As May and I opened the door of the coop, we saw William laying on an old bunk that was situated against the window on the left-hand side of the shack. Brady was sitting on a bunk that ran parallel to it, pushed against the right wall. Laying on the beach, I could suddenly recall the overpowering stench of the chickens that had previously resided there; I'd stood breathing in the suffocating heat of the summer as we opened up the door to reveal what was inside. Brady and William were approximately thirteen or fourteen at the time, and they were busy looking at some magazines on their respective bunks. We were not expected guests, and they were surprised by our arrival. At our appearance, they immediately engaged us to show them our private parts for a nickel or two. I remember discussing the offer with May, and she refused and was encouraging me to do the same thing. I ignored my sister's warning and walked toward Brady to accept the nickel that he was offering with his now outstretched hand. As I approached him, he stood up and grabbed me and forced me onto his bunk face-down. My pants were swiftly pulled down and then I felt the pain of his body entering mine, and my mind entered a shattered place that I had never experienced before. All these years later, I remembered crying the type of cry that constricted your lungs and where breathing was difficult between gasps for air.

The next thing I knew, my mother was at the doorway screaming, "They have damaged her for life!" I heard her repeat those words over and over again, and also say that no man would ever want me. She took me in her arms and carried me the short distance to our house. She rocked and held me for a long time before telephoning her sister to tell her what had happened. This would be one of the only times in my life where I would remember my mother holding me so tightly as she did that day. That day would remain one of the only times in my life when I could remember her caring so deeply for my well-being.

This all came rolling back to me as though it had just happened yesterday.

Of course, I was no longer in any relaxed state on my beach towel, but had taken an upright sitting position to stare out into the open sea as if it might offer some answers. My mind raced as I tried to make sense of things that I had wondered about over the years, and to process the memory. Brady and his sisters had mysteriously disappeared from our lives, no explanation given for why they no longer came to visit or why we no longer went to their home. The entire family had disappeared from town, in fact, and I'd never known why. I had enjoyed the company of Brady and his sisters in the past, and couldn't understand why nobody had informed me about their whereabouts.

And there was also a painful visit to the doctor's office, after which I recalled him looking at my private area with a painful instrument, and a strange conversation with my mother that followed and which I didn't understand. I remembered that doctor as being very kind, and got a lollipop despite my tears.

Even as life had gone forward with some confusions, I'd apparently managed to lose the day that had caused it all, until this day at the beach.

It would not be until I was in my late forties that I would have the courage to ask May about this incident, and she acknowledged that it had actually occurred. May shared with me that she was the one who fetched my mother that day to come to my rescue, as she tried hard to be my protector. My brother William didn't seem to care about what had happened to me. He made no attempts to stop Brady from sexually abusing me, and was obviously just an enabler. Whether he was reprimanded later on for his participation, I don't know and probably will never know. Even now, I don't know why he didn't interfere and physically stop Brady; I didn't even hear him protesting, truth be told. All these years later, William has never made any mention of the incident, and we have never talked about that day in the chicken coop. Strangely, though our relationship has periodically been strained over the years, I seem to be the one family member who he regularly keeps in touch with.

After May, though, it was my mother who I wanted to speak to about all of this. In my late forties, I desperately wanted to have a conversation with my mother about that day, but could just never manage to start the conversation. I would plan my attempts, but would always stop myself from proceeding. As you'll soon understand, my mother was not always as attentive as she should have been during our childhood years – this made the conversation harder to even begin. As children, we could play for hours outside, and she would never come and check on us. Compounding this problem, my father was at one point absent for almost a year due to back surgery as a result of an injury that he'd received while working. It was during his absence that this event in my life had occurred.

Looking back, I believe that it was as a result of this physical trauma to my body that I also developed a bladder problem. I started wetting my pants at the most inconvenient of times. May knew that I had no control once I would start to laugh about something, and my bladder would just leak out all of its contents. It was a very embarrassing situation to have – especially when an outsider would learn of the problem. My family physician couldn't find any physical cause, and suggested that I wear Kotex pads until I grew out of it. May would take every opportunity to make me laugh in order to cause me to wet my pants. She coined me with the nickname of "Peecat" and called me that many times throughout my childhood. Over time, I became an expert at covering up my wet pants with a jacket or sneaking into the house after I had an "accident" in my father's car. My parents never made an issue of the fact that I had this problem and never reprimanded me for any wetting incidents, and I've since wondered if they knew that it was a result of Brady's intrusion on my body, that that caused the physical complication, and they felt responsible.

At the time, of course, I did not understand my mother's words in regards to my having been damaged, and then I forgot them for so many years anyway. Since the memory has come back to me, though, I've come to think of myself as having been blemished. I've learned that most people have been marked by some event in their life. Some people have been marked in a physical way and they have visible scars to show the damage. I was somehow marked emotionally, and only finally was I made aware of the scar. When I remembered, I was horrified that my innocence had been taken at such an early age. I didn't realize at the time that this new knowledge would make an impact on me, both subconsciously and consciously, affecting my future relationships with men.

I had trusted both Brady and my brother, you see, and I suddenly wondered why neither one of them had cared about me. Did my brother William now despise me because he'd lost his best friend when they'd moved out of town? He had been an observer of the loss of my innocence. Did he feel guilty for his lack of caring about my well-being? He was my older brother and he was supposed to have been my protector, but instead he'd been just an observer. Why did he not speak up and say something to Brady? Why did he not care about me in the way that my mother and sister cared? I was his little sister, I thought, and he was supposed to look out for me.

I now had a lot to think about that summer at the Jersey shore, but I wondered why this memory had waited for so long to appear. Why did my mind wait until I was hundreds of miles away from home and on my own to make me aware of a memory that had been living inside of me for the past sixteen years?

And yet, the new knowledge didn't define my summer because so much happened in the way of new relationships. I made some new friends and was living at the seashore, as I had planned. And, since I had no one to talk to about this painful discovery, I managed to decide to just push it back inside the area of my mind from where it had escaped – for the moment, at least.

Back to the present moment... I stood up from my beach towel to walk into the warm salt water, as if to wash off the memory that had stunned me with its newly offered awareness. As I walked back to the small apartment that I now shared with nine other girls, I felt like I was a totally different person than I'd been earlier in the day. I had just moved some small belongings into that apartment a few days earlier. The tiny living space was situated on a second floor above the scenic boardwalk. It was set up to provide free living arrangements for the summer employees of three custard stands that were spread across the long boardwalk. It hadn't been the type of employment that I'd had in mind when I left my small town in Pennsylvania, I admit. I had set out to find a job in a local bank or some small industry where I could have a career and make some real money. Instead, I'd landed on the boardwalk with a summer job as a server of custard and ice cold lemon drinks, and somehow, I was grateful for the employment and free living space. I had left my home with only a small amount of money and wasn't sure how far it was going to extend. I had already paid out three hundred dollars to a creepy old man to rent a dingy apartment. And though I'd tried to retrieve that money after securing my current position, he wouldn't return it to me. Still inexperience in such matters, I wasn't aware at the time that I could have just cancelled the check through my bank.

But, luckily, I met Carl Mancini – the manager of the stand where I was to spend the summer working. He was a short stalky gentleman who hired me on the spot and immediately introduced me to my fellow employees. The other girls in the apartment were a bit more street-smart than myself, being from New York and New Jersey. I had grown up in a rural community where everyone knew everyone else, and I had never spent any time at all in a larger city. All of the girls seemed as though they had city roots and might not have been as naïve about the ways of the world as I was. I wasn't sure how I was going to fit into the small confines of that living space when I moved in, truth be told. I chose a room that had three small cots and I chose the bed that was in the middle. There was no sitting space in the unit, but it had a small kitchen with limited working space and two bathrooms to be shared between us. There was no radio or television set, and we were pretty isolated from what was happening in the world.

I walked a lot that summer, up and down the boardwalk, eating food from the various eateries along the way. My diet mostly consisted of pizza slices and sneak tastes of custard and other delights when Carl wasn't around. The girls who I was living with liked to party almost every night, but I wasn't as interested in it I spent a lot of time reading instead, both at the beach and on my small cot, to pass any free time that I had. I would occasionally join the others at a local bar, but always felt out of place because I didn't really enjoy getting drunk.

About a month into my stay, I became friendly with a fellow roommate who was named Sue. Out of all the girls I'd met, she seemed to have more of the small- town traits that I could readily identify with at the time. I was shy and reserved, and sometimes found it hard to make friends. I held some secrets from my past and didn't really wish to reveal them to anyone, for fear of being judged. But, Sue and I would walk on the beach and enjoy the sun and the sand. On occasion, she would convince me to go out to some rowdy joint right on the boardwalk, not far from our housing.

One of the other girls that we lived with was very unique. She was unlike anyone else I had ever met in her looks as well as her behavior. Her name was Monica and she had a disease called AIDS (which was barely known at that time, at least where I came from). The day that I first met Monica, she was dressed in some very unusual clothing that was put together as a sort of futuristic type of attire. She had on some bright red high top sneakers with striped shorts and suspenders to match. She had long dark brown hair with colorful spectacles that were overly large in shape and which outweighed the small features of her face. Extremely skinny and tanned, she still had an unhealthy appearance, but it was offset by her outgoing personality and a very distinct New York accent. Upon meeting us, she told all of us that she did not feel well, and that she had the AIDS virus. Truthfully, I wasn't frightened by her, but I knew that she was very different looking than anyone else I had ever met. I could also sense that she was a free spirit, and I had never encountered anyone quite like her before.

Monica quickly bonded with one of the other girls, Robin, who told us that her mother was a nurse and so she was familiar with the AIDS virus. Robin had a very holistic and healthy look about herself, and was a complete contrast to Monica. Her cheeks were rosy and her white teeth gleamed against her creamy white skin. Her dark brown hair was cut in the shape of a neat bob, and she really looked like she could have been a nurse herself. Monica and Robin came from the same part of New York and immediately became best friends, helped along by the fact that Robin immediately showed great compassion for Monica. After we learned Monica had AIDS, Robin just plopped down on the cot beside her and placed her arm around her shoulders, as if to say everything was going to be alright. I wondered how a stranger could care so much for another person almost instantly. She did not seem to have any concern for her own health in regards to the virus. Personally, I had never even heard of the disease before, and didn't feel any great concern in regards to my own personal health either. Some of the other housemates seemed to know more about it, and quietly expressed some concern amongst themselves. My thoughts were elsewhere. I wasn't sure why Monica was working at a custard stand when she obviously didn't seem to be feeling well. My thoughts revolved around her family, and why she wasn't in her home and being cared for by them.

In the first few weeks of our living together, Monica's health seemed to decline and it became difficult for her to get out of bed in the morning and get to work, as she was sometimes quite ill. She managed to go off in the evenings to party with the other girls, and I just assumed that she had too much to drink. I continued to witness Robin showing Monica great concern each time she would become gravely ill, though, and I was amazed at how someone who was not a family member could care so much about someone after such a short period of time.

Not long after Monica displayed real signs of illness, I found myself unprepared for what was about to happen amongst the ladies in our living quarters. A few of the girls had discovered more information about AIDS and demanded that something be done about the place that we were living in. The ladies said that we were all contaminated, and had made complaints to the owners of the custard stand. In response, the owners asked Monica to leave the unit, and we were told that we needed to wash and sanitize all of our belongings, as well as discard our toiletries. At this point in time, we had been sharing this living space for the last two months, and I figured that we were already contaminated. I was just not sure with what I had been contaminated, if at all. Still, I lugged all of my belongings out of the apartment with the rest of the girls and made my way to the laundromat. I had never seen such drama as what I witnessed at the laundromat, though! My roommates were screaming and yelling at each other about how we were all infected with the AIDS virus, and that we were all going to die from the disease. I had never been involved in such a hate-filled environment in my life, and it was all directed toward Monica and Robin. Robin was disgusted with all of us, and had gathered her belongings and left with Monica. Where they went, I'll never know, because they just disappeared without any goodbyes.

Throughout the summer, we had all worked rotating shifts, and sometimes verbal battles had taken place while I was out of the apartment. I had kept to myself and just seemed to be an observant outsider, but now I was a participant in the aftermath. I didn't know who was involved in the accusations, though, and I wasn't even quite sure of the series of events that had led up to us marching to the laundromat! While we were out of the apartment, it was thoroughly cleaned by an outside cleaning company and we were told that it was safe to reenter the unit. You have to remember that, at this time, there were a lot of myths going around about AIDS, and the average person just didn't know much about it – beyond that it existed, if that.

Meanwhile, upon our return to the apartment, the tension remained quite high, and division amongst its tenants was evident in some of the rude comments being sent back and forth. I was somehow able to keep a clear head and mind about the situation by keeping my thoughts to myself.

To add to the chaos, Sue had recently discovered that she was pregnant, and so she had concerns that she *and* her baby had been infected with the AIDS virus. She had screamed at Monica during her exit from the apartment and had made some especially hateful remarks in that regard. I'd been embarrassed to be associated with her, I was so surprised at her reaction to the news. At that point, I saw a side of her personality that I hadn't been aware of and didn't like very much. She asked me if I would consider moving with her to another apartment, she was so upset, and in my empathy for her situation I showed her the apartment that I had originally intended to live in. She found it to be small and dreary as well, and neither one of us wanted to spend the money involved in staying there for one last month of employment. I was also hesitant to live with her at all, as I had seen how her emotions could get out of control.

Some things were looking up, though. Just prior to all of the commotion, I had received a job offer to teach school in the school district that I'd grown up in, serving as a permanent substitute teacher for the upcoming fall semester. I'd accepted the offer and was planning to return to my small town at the end of the summer. My father had called several times over the past few weeks, and had encouraged me to come home early since I had a job lined up for the fall. After all of the theatrics that had taken place, I finally decided to give Carl my two weeks' notice and head home. I just wanted to forget the recent events and move forward in my new career.

I had enjoyed living so close to the beach and the serene feel of the ocean just outside of my door, but the happenings inside that apartment I occupied were sometimes not so serene, and had eventually been filled with a lack of compassion for someone who was suffering with a horrible disease. That said, I have to add that I didn't understand the dynamics of the disease until a few years later when it reached epidemic proportions and gained more headlines. Had I understood the disease while living in that apartment, I guess I may have had a different reaction to living with someone who was infected. At the time, I was so different from the other girls that it was as though I was a stranger living amongst them, witnessing the unfair treatment of Monica. It wasn't until years later that I realized that AIDS was a serious life and death condition, and that I had encountered one of its earliest victims. I felt bad then that I hadn't shown her more empathy and concern at the time, and also, I realized that Monica was marked, as well. She was damaged by a disease that instilled fear in people. That fear would swell in numbers as the AIDS epidemic would sweep around the world.

On my long drive back to my hometown, I thought about my summer at the Jersey Shore. I knew that I was a different person than the one who had arrived only a few months earlier. It was the summer of the discovery of a wound that I was wearing in my heart. I wondered if my wound would go away and become a forgotten scar.

A few months later, I heard from Sue that she'd had a baby girl and that it was fine. She had also heard through one of our previous roommates that Monica had passed away. I knew in my heart that she had been wounded by her roommates' reactions, and might have had a scar from even that summer that never went away.

That summer served me as a rude awakening in many respects. I realized that I had been in a situation similar to that of my brother William. I was also an onlooker in a situation where I could have used my voice to speak up for an injustice. Why did I not have the courage to speak up about what was occurring in the apartment where I resided? I also wondered why I didn't have the same type of compassion which Robin had held for Monica. And how did a complete stranger give Monica more compassion than she apparently received from her own family members? My mother had been there for me when I'd needed her, and I wondered about Monica's relationship with her own mother. Why was her mother not there for her?

Hopefully, Monica was able to bond with her mother prior to her passing. I hoped that, in the future, I would care enough about others to speak up about any injustice I saw – regardless of whether they were related to me or not. Just like Brady and his family, my fellow roommates disappeared from my life. I'd only had those few moments of time to make a difference in someone else's life, and they'd only had a few moments to make a difference in mine.

My Mother

In thinking about Monica and her relationship with her mother, I started to really think about my own relationship with my mother and what had made her the person that she had become. The love that I have for my mother is not lacking, but it misses a closeness that I have witnessed amongst other mothers and daughters. I've sometimes thought that maybe it has something to do with the way that my mother was raised. She lost her father suddenly, when she was five years old. Possibly, her father's passing left a permanent blemish on her and her family, and I speculated as to whether I would confront similar situations as a result of my own blemish. Without warning, her father had been struck on the head with a baseball bat while acting as a spectator at a baseball game. He was immediately rushed to the hospital, where he passed away later that same evening. This fateful event left my mother and her four sisters without a father – in a time when the economy was suffering from the great depression. My mother and I are very similar in that we both had something tragic happen to us at the same time in our lives. I've wondered if that event spawned some of the problems that she would encounter throughout her lifetime.

My grandfather's passing left my grandmother and her four daughters without an income in a difficult time period. She struggled with raising my mother and her four sisters by doing laundry, ironing, housecleaning, and other similar jobs. And, my mother and her sisters went to work at an early age to help with the household budget. To tell you about my grandmother... Grandma Betty was a wonderful cook and housekeeper. Betty wore nylons, black Mary

Jane shoes, and always had on a dress with a clean white apron. Her constant companion was a dog named Tina who was not fixed and was constantly being a nuisance on our legs. Grandma was a seemingly quiet woman and she was very fond of me in an unspoken kind of way, and I was very fond of her.

She would call our home almost every day and ask to speak to my mother. Yet, my mother would ask us to tell her that she was not at home. I could not and would not lie to my grandmother, though, and so I would get reprimanded for not obeying my mother's orders. I just couldn't understand why one would not want to speak to their own mother on the telephone. My mother didn't work at the time either, so I knew that my grandmother would wonder where she could possibly have gone to on a daily basis. Truth be told, I didn't understand the relationship between my mother and grandmother then, and I still don't.

However, in observing the relationship between my grandmother and my mother, I have to say that they seemed to be lacking in the same type of closeness that's always been missing between myself and my mother. My mother had an aloofness about her that made getting close difficult, as she was sometimes emotionally elusive. If you tried to pin her down, she would purposefully change the subject. My grandmother, on the other hand, was direct with her, and I felt that my mother avoided her for that reason. I also questioned my mother about her lack of response to her own mother, and got a similar reaction.

Thinking back, I've likened my grandmother to a mother bird checking on a wounded member of the flock, as she just wanted to make sure that my mother was alright. Even if it was with a daily phone call, as she did not call her other daughters on such a regular basis. It is also possible that my mother found it tiresome to have someone checking on her all the time.

When I was a senior in high school, I saw my mother show the same type of distant emotional behavior toward my grandmother in regards to her end-of-life care. My grandmother had never remarried after the loss of her husband, and remained in the home that she had always loved for as long as her daughters would permit her to do so. It was with great sadness that I watched her daughters place my grandmother in a nursing home. After a bout with pneumonia and a hospital stay at the age of eighty-four, though, she could no longer manage the stairs in her two-story home. It had also become very difficult for her to bathe and dress on her own. My sister and I took turns spending the night in our grandma's home to be with her in case she needed some help, but the daughters eventually decided (and with relative ease) that my grandmother needed to go into a nursing home and put her home up for sale. It was against my grandmother's will, despite her difficulties, and she was not happy with the decision. It was made known to all her family members that she wanted to die in her own home. During my weekly visits to the nursing home, it pained me to see my grandmother strapped down to her bed, and I could not understand the cruelty – at the time, it was the way things were done, simply to keep my grandmother from leaving her bed, but there was no way for me to view it as anything but cruel. My grandmother would cry to me to get her out of there and to take her home. I could only imagine the sadness that she would feel if she knew of the plans to sell her beloved home. It was such an awful sight to see, and I felt so very helpless in the situation.

I could not understand how my mother could not listen to her own mother's pleas to be released from that horrible place. My mother would instead sit by emotionlessly as Grandma Betty lay flat on her bed, strapped down with restraints so that she was unable to get up. She wanted to escape that awful place, so they had to keep her movement restricted. I was so disappointed with my mother and her sisters, in that they did nothing to help her, and they were keeping her in such a place. I wanted to take her home with us, but my mother told me that we could not because we could not take care of her.

It broke my heart to see her in such distress, and I knew that my grandmother would surely lose her will to live in that type of situation. It didn't seem to me that there would *be* much reason to continue living like that. My grandmother was very angry, and I did not blame her because she had lived in that house almost her entire life. She simply wanted to die in her own home, and I felt that she had the right to do so. I would leave that nursing home with a sour pit in my stomach each time we visited, just thinking about my grandmother being left all alone in that place. She'd been placed in the nursing home at the beginning of June, and she passed away in the middle of the night in the heat of a late August evening. As strange as it may seem, I woke up in the middle of the night that night, and I could feel her presence in my bedroom, and I felt that she had come to visit with me one last time. It was only a few moments later that my mother received the call that she had passed.

My grandmother's funeral was a sad occasion for my sister and me. Our minister delivered the service and I sobbed with great sadness. I don't remember that my mother shed a single tear at that service, but I know that she was heavily medicated. Her lack of emotion still made me question her care and concern for my grandmother, but I was quick to excuse her because I knew about her problems.

During World War II, my mother and all of her sisters worked in a factory that made hand grenades which were then shipped overseas. Later on, my mother also worked in a sewing machine factory for a short time, sewing girdles and brassieres. Once she married my father, she became a stay at home mom. My father was the type of man who enjoyed taking care of my mother and making sure that all of her needs were met. He was a tall and handsome man with a full head of hair that framed his suntanned face. His face was weather-beaten from working out in the sun, but was seamlessly free of wrinkles. Both of my parents somehow managed to keep their youthful looks well into their seventies, due to their wholesome lifestyle.

My parents raised what seemed like two sets of children. They had my two older brothers, Martin who is twelve years older than myself and William who was born four years after Martin. I was born seven years after William, and then my sister came along shortly afterwards.

In her younger years, my mother had a full head of long dark chocolate hair, and almond shaped hazel eyes with full lips. She was a beautiful woman with a shapely figure that was very appealing to the eye. She was the only one in our family who was petite, as all of her children towered over her five-foot-four frame.

Early on, my sister and I had beautiful dresses, capes, and hats to wear, as my mother had become a beautiful and talented seamstress. Every religious holiday, we had a newly sewn outfit to wear to church. While I was in grade school, she made several attempts to teach me how to sew, but, quite frankly, I was a tomboy and I was more interested in playing outside. By the time I was in junior high school, I finally did show some interest in learning, but suddenly she would not be in the mood to teach me. She also made a lot of her own clothes and had a closet full of items that she'd purchased at the expensive department stores. The only place that she wore most of them was to our local church on Sunday. My father never denied her anything within reason, despite his modest income.

During our earlier years, she paid a lot of attention to our clothing and to making sure we were well taken care of. Once we entered junior high school, though, things seemed to have changed, as May and I started sharing our clothes and shoes. Our clothing allotment became very limited as our mother's seemed to expand. She no longer made our clothes at all, and our visits to the department store for shopping were to fill up her own closet.

Not only was she interested in her own clothing, but she always impressed upon us to never leave the house without wearing lipstick. She never left the house without a full face of makeup, and her hair was always in place. Her instructions must have left an impression because, to this day, I never leave the house without lipstick and I even wear it to the gym. She was quite devout in the care of her hair also, and would make a weekly trip to the beauty salon to get her hair done. For many of my earlier years, my mother didn't drive, so my father had to leave work to take her to regular beauty salon appointments. The end of the world could be coming, and she would still have to get her hair done. Sometimes heated discussions would arise revolving around those hair appointments and my father's work agenda.

When my mother was not tending to her hair, she spent some time in the kitchen. As with most things, she would have to be in the mood to cook or bake, and she was usually in a good mood when she was doing either task. It seemed as though it was something that she really did enjoy.

Just like Grandma Betty, she was an excellent cook, and some of my fondest memories revolved around the kitchen, when she was making homemade apple pies. I enjoyed watching her roll out the pie dough and then use the left-over remnants for apple dumplings. My sister and I would sit at the kitchen table and watch her roll out the dough with what seemed like perfection. We would entertain each other with lively chatter as she went through the steps of putting the pie together, and we would eat apple slices dipped in sugar and cinnamon. She received lots of compliments for the wonderful apple pies that she made. It was a recipe that I am sure she learned from her mother.

Making pies, though, was about the most normal activity in our household when I was growing up. Nothing else was ever what you would call "normal". My mother was diagnosed as being a paranoid schizophrenic when I was thirteen years old. She had demonstrated symptoms of her disease prior to that timeframe, but had never officially been diagnosed. I knew that there was something not quite right with her, and a description of her illness appearing in a school textbook finally defined it for me. It was not long after she threatened to take her own life that an official diagnosis was made.

One weekend, she isolated herself in her bedroom and didn't come out for days on end. I don't know what the events were that led up to this complete emotional breakdown on her part, but she cried for several days, only leaving the confines of her bedroom to use the bathroom, despite coaxing from my father, my sister, and myself. (My brothers were no longer living with us, as they'd graduated from high school and had moved out.) Isolating herself, my mother refused to come downstairs to eat dinner with us, and declined the attempts my sister and I made to deliver trays of food to her bedroom door. She told all of us – including my father – to "go away". At the time, I couldn't understand why she didn't want to eat and why she didn't want to be around us. After my father's many gentle attempts to speak with her, he finally called two of her sisters to come to the house, this being just after she threatened to kill herself with an overdose of aspirin. He was at his wits' end when he thought to enlist their help. They managed to encourage her to go to the hospital, where she was committed for the first time to the mental ward. This would be the first of many trips there that she would make over the years.

Upon learning about the diagnosis of her disease, there was almost a relief felt – that they had a name for her condition and that it was not just my imagination that there was something very unusual about her.

There were many moments throughout our childhood when May and I would come home from school to find that she was nowhere to be found until we opened a closet door. She would be sitting inside the dark closet on a large pretzel tin that we had received for a holiday gift. We would ask her what she was doing in the closet, and she would tell us that "she was praying" and to "please shut the door". May would then do some mocking imitation or make a funny comment in order to make me laugh. My sister and I used laughter a lot to deal with my mother's strange behavior.

May and I would sometimes come home from school in a good mood, and with expectations of my mother waiting with homemade cookies to greet us… only to find her sitting in a closet and wanting to be alone, or just staring off into space from the living room sofa. She would later emerge from her thoughts as though her actions had been nothing unusual. I often wondered what she was praying or thinking about, and why she found it necessary to sit in a dark closet, but either way, I quickly realized that arriving home from school was always going to be an adventure of imbalance. Sometimes, it's true, she would surprise us with a treat and things seemed as though they were just like any other family, but I came to realize that she had variable moods, and she peculiar, odd thoughts that would manipulate her mind and ultimately put her in a dark place. In those times, I would walk on eggshells around her in order to avoid listening to some strange conversation about how someone had done something to her. Her paranoid thoughts that someone was trying to kill her, or that

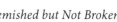

the world was coming to an end; she would create imaginary themes around my father having unfounded affairs with neighbor ladies. Absurd thoughts burdened her mind about some person not liking her, and how they were out to undermine her in some way. The ones regarding someone trying to undermine her sometimes tickled me because she would choose someone who she didn't even interact with on a daily basis. It was typically another churchgoer or neighbor lady who she would choose as her nemesis. I would try to tell her it wasn't true and ask her how she knew it to be the truth, but the answers she would provide had no foundation, and she had no facts to justify her answers. A typical response to my inquiry would be "just because". After this type of conversation would take place, I would generally escape to my bedroom to find some peace of mind by listening to music or reading.

I will admit that, when she first started to talk about the end of the world coming, she instilled some fear in me. She faithfully read her Bible and repeated verses out of the Book of Revelations, and I sometimes thought that maybe she could be onto something. My father would reassure me that it was not the case, though, and that I needn't worry about her concerns. Yet, at various later moments in my life, I would sometimes find myself having feelings of impending gloom and doom, and think that they were somehow related to my having always been on the ready for the end of the world at this earlier point in my life.

In my early twenties when she would start these types of conversations, I would subsequently get a sickening feeling in my stomach and find them to be very disturbing to listen to. I would think to myself, "Here we go again." Paranoid conversations would typically be one of the first indicators that she was not taking her medications and that, if she were not careful, she would be going back to the mental institution.

One such instance occurred when I was home from my second year in college, in the summer of 1978. My father had arranged for a long weekend in August to go to Virginia Beach with my mother to play golf. Both of my parents enjoyed golfing and it was a fun activity for them to do together. He had booked a hotel right on the ocean so that they could also enjoy the beach after a morning of golf. The second morning after they had arrived, I received a phone call from my father. He was in tears as he told me that my mother had gotten in the car and left him there all alone. The only other time that I had heard my father cry was at his father's funeral, and I knew that he was in shock about what had just taken place, and left with no idea in regards to her possible whereabouts. My father needed my older brother to go and pick him up, and still, he was not sure where my mother had gone... but knew that she had been talking about the end of the world.

In the weeks prior to their getaway, my mother had stopped taking her daily medications and my father had been gravely concerned. My mother going for long bouts without her medication was never a good thing. Trying to get her to take her medication, though, was always an uphill battle, as she did not think that she needed it. My father had often held private discussions with us in regards to how to get her to take her medicine, and this time his thinking had been that taking her on a getaway might help to remedy the situation, in that she would get a change of scenery to redirect her thoughts.

In the days that led up to their trip, however, she'd felt as though the world was going to come to an end and had wanted us to be prepared. My mother started to assemble our downstairs basement as a bomb shelter by stocking the shelves with tons of canned goods. She had my father purchase several huge garbage cans which were then placed in the basement so that my mother could fill them with water. We had a large, deep freezer, and that got moved to the basement, as well. Disturbing conversations at dinnertime revolved around the impending end of the world and how we needed to be organized. Along with these talks came other accusations about how my father was having an affair, and that he wanted to get rid of her.

The assembling for the end of the world had been going on for the entirety of that summer. As much as one would like to be prepared for any event, of course, there was no preparation for the phone call that I received from my father after my mother disappeared from that weekend getaway. At the time, I wasn't sure for which parent to be most concerned. I think I felt sorry for my father being stranded somewhere without a car and without his wife. But truthfully, most of my concern was for my mother and her driving habits. The distance which she would have to travel was well over seven hours, and through some heavily congested traffic areas which she had never navigated.

My mother was not a cautious driver, and I simply couldn't imagine her driving from Virginia back to our small town in Pennsylvania all alone. May was not home at the time, and I called to inform her of our mother's disappearance. I couldn't quite believe that my mother had left my father, and I was irritated with her for leaving him behind. I was also concerned for her safety as I tried to imagine where she could possibly have gone. I wondered if she was on her way home, or if she had plans to go somewhere else, and if I would ever see her again.

You see, I knew how she drove. Riding in the car with her as the driver was a terrifying experience, and we would often argue over who was going to drive. It was only when I was learning how to drive the family car at the age of sixteen that my mother also obtained her driver's license, then being at the age of fifty-two. She'd never gotten her driver's license because her own mother had never learned how to drive. They didn't have a car when she was growing up, and always had to rely on other people for transportation. And when my mother married my father, he took her everywhere that she needed to go. At the time when I was learning how to drive, though, my mother encouraged my father to teach her, as well. Why she waited till it was my time to learn how to drive was puzzling to me, and I remember feeling like she was in some type of competition with me for my father's attention. Every time that I wanted my father to take me out driving, she insisted that he take her first. I passed my test first, though, and it took her three trying times prior to her passing her test.

I remember that she felt that everyone should stop their car for her as she would pull out of an intersection. Several times, I dropped to the floor of the backseat because I was sure that we were going to be in an accident and that I needed to protect myself. On one occasion, she almost ran over an elderly gentleman who was walking with a cane, in a crosswalk right in front of us! Angry, he hit the front hood of our car with his cane after the near miss and screamed at her to "slow down." I didn't blame him one bit for being irritated. May and I later shared this story with our father, and we could tell that he was worried about her driving abilities.

Truth be told, it was very evident that my mother felt that she was more important than anyone else when she was driving the car. Why she felt this way, I don't know. She certainly had no concern for the well-being of her passengers, who were her children, let alone the safety of other drivers.

So, as you can imagine, it was with much concern that I waited to see if my mother would arrive safely back from Virginia – if that was even her intention. Without any word by telephone from anyone all day, I nervously paced around the house. I was left alone in our home for the evening and alone with my fears. It was finally around eight o'clock that same evening when she proudly pranced into our home, holding her Bible in her arms. I immediately confronted her with questions regarding the whereabouts of my father and why she'd left him behind. I was furious with her then, not only because of her answer but because of her self-righteous attitude. She told me that the world was coming to an end, as the waves had been coming into shore rather high on the beach. She told me that she'd indicated to my father that she did not want to stay there, so she'd just gotten up that next morning and gotten in the car and left him! I was quite angry with her, and asked her how she could do such a thing. I could feel myself trembling as I waited for her response. And at first, she made no response at all as she walked away from me. Walking towards another room in our home, she didn't answer my question, but she finally turned around to look at me and told me that she'd "put her Bible under her feet and the good Lord and angels got her home safely". Knowing her driving record and the fact that she had to drive around the Washington D.C. beltway, I knew that someone had gotten her home safely. Now, as to whether it was the good Lord or the angels, that I was not quite sure of.

During the course of this conversation, I could not believe that she didn't even ask about my father and how he was going to get home. It was painfully obvious to me that she had no concerns about anybody except herself, and I wanted to scold her for her lack of concern about her husband and my father... but I didn't want to get into an argument with her. I just didn't understand how someone could do such a thing to their spouse, who was so devout in taking care of them.

That evening, I retreated to my bedroom in order to avoid her and any further discussion about her thoughtless behavior. My brother and my father arrived home the following day. With verbal resistance and some crying, my mother was again taken to the hospital by my father and brother, and once again she was admitted to the mental ward.

This was not the only time that I confronted my mother so directly, but this particular incident would remain in my mind even years later due to the intensity of our confrontation. The extreme emotional reactions between the two of us were of a greater magnitude at that particular time than nearly ever before. Truth be told, challenging my mother about anything always got my stomach in a knot. It could almost feel traumatic. The most disquieting face-off of all, though, had happened just prior to the time leading up to my sixth-grade graduation party. My sister May can still recall all the details of the argument that ensued between us. The graduation party was going to be my first school dance, and of course there was a lot of excitement buzzing around the topic at school. I was looking forward to the dance and I was having discussions with my classmates about the outfits that we would all be wearing for such a grand occasion.

One evening prior to the dance, I approached my mother while she had her ironing board set up in the kitchen and, in one of her rare working moments, was ironing some clothes. I had just completed washing and drying the evening dishes, and now I broached the subject of a new outfit to wear to the dance. Her response was not what I'd expected, as she proceeded to tell me that I would not be getting a new outfit for the dance. When I asked her why, her response was one that sent my self-confidence floundering – because she told me that all of my friends did not like me, and that they were not really my friends at all. She said that I was not the popular person who I thought that I was, and that if she were me, that she would not even attend the dance. I exploded with rebuttals for her remarks, arguing that they were not true, that my friends didn't feel that way about me. She continued to argue back that it was true, and that my best friend at the time did not even like me. I was so taken aback and surprised that I was immediately brought to tears, and so I found myself shouting back at her, responding to her false accusations. I couldn't believe that my own mother was spewing such hateful comments to me, that were surely meant to be hurtful. This argument went back and forth for what seemed like hours as I watched her mouth and face become distorted in anger and she continued to focus on her ironing. She would not even look at me as tears streamed down my face and we each tried to justify our positions. Her talking pushed upon me feelings of doubt in regards to my friendships at school, and I wondered if she knew something about them that I didn't know. None of this had ever been previously mentioned, and I wondered why she was telling me all this now. Why did she choose this moment to take a shot at my self-confidence?

My sister was in the dining room right next to the country kitchen, listening intently to the entire incident since she dared not come into the room. Just when I thought that the conversation could not continue any longer, though, my father arrived home from his evening chores. He came into the room and demanded to know, "What's going on in here?" I thought that I was going to be in trouble with him, as well. But to my surprise, after just a few seconds, he told my mother to "stop it" and for me to go upstairs to my room. I wasted no time in exiting and May followed quickly behind me as we went up to my parents' bedroom, where we could try and listen through the heat register to the conversation below. My father was attempting to calm her down and he was having a difficult time. There were some heated words between them, but the conversation finally came to an end. We hadn't heard any of it very clearly, though, and didn't know how it all came to an end.

The next weekend, my parents took me shopping to a local department store where we purchased a dark brown suede vest with strands of fringe decorating the bottom. I was pleased with the purchase and delighted to have something fun to wear to the dance. The evening of the dance came, and I twirled the night away with the fringe on my vest swinging around on the dance floor of the stage in our dated school cafeteria. I was surrounded by my grade school friends and it was one of the most fun and carefree times that I have ever had in my life. The doubts that my mother had created in regards to my friendships seemed to dissipate for the moment. But while it was not evident at the dance, the hateful remarks that she'd made in regards to my friendships somehow added a longstanding blemish to my self-confidence. I *had* won the battle with my mother, in the fact that I got the new outfit to wear to the dance, but not without a cost. Was she really that hateful, to want to damage my self-confidence, or was she just jealous that she herself did not have any lasting friendships?

It was only those few times when I really stood up to my mother's seemingly cold disposition and lack of caring for anyone but herself. It sometimes took everything I had inside me to dispute her disposition. Simply, having a mother with a mental illness has not always been a picnic. Regardless, we somehow managed to have some good times together as a family. It was sometimes difficult to keep our roles in life in mind, of course, but she was my mother and I did love her in spite of her strange changes in mood. Over the years, I learned how to best deal with her moods and personality changes. I knew that I could not take anything personally, as the next day everything could be quite different from the day prior. It took some time, but I finally came to the realization that her disease was just that – a disease – and that arguing with her would not get you anywhere.

It was the type of disease, however, that you wanted to conceal from the world – because of the stigma associated with mental illness.

Our family tried hard to keep her problem amongst ourselves and our relatives. However, we lived in a small town, and word about "her problem" eventually became a newsworthy event.

The summer after leaving my father in Virginia, she stopped taking her medication once again, which resulted in her actually disappearing on us. One late July day in the summer of 1979, she took the family car and went to the beauty shop for her weekly permanent or wash and set. After her visit at the salon, she went to the local bank and withdrew all the money from my father's savings account for which she was the co-owner. Without a word to anyone, she then drove to a nearby town and applied for a gun permit. Instead of returning home, she then checked herself into a local hotel where she proceeded to camp out. We had no idea where she'd gone and, when she did not return home that Friday afternoon, we contacted her hairdresser and then the local sheriff. Several days passed, and when she still did not return home, information regarding her whereabouts was sought via the local news channels and the local paper. The news media identified her as a person with a mental illness and provided her photograph. It was now out into the community that my mother had a mental illness, and public knowledge.

Growing up, I'd been fearful that others would learn about her disease, and had thought that they would surely not have any depth of understanding about our situation. It was with much caution that I had invited people into our home, for fear of some embarrassing misbehavior that she might commit. I was never sure what she was going to say or do, and wanted to avoid any embarrassing consequences, so I never felt comfortable having my friends over for a sleep-over or even for dinner. She'd rarely attend any of the important school events that my sister or I were involved in, though May and I were very active on several high school sports teams; yet, she only came to see our games once or twice during the four years that we were involved. She did come to my high school graduation, but not to my induction into the honor society. At times, I was honestly relieved that she wasn't present at important events because it freed me from worry over any incident causing her to misbehave socially.

There were periods of time during my high school years when she lived like a recluse, other than to get her hair done. I often wondered why she was getting her hair done at all when no one was going to see her except her own family.

Most of her episodes of inappropriate behavior revolved around the small church to which we belonged. During her sporadic attendance, she would get up out of her pew in the middle of the sermon and stomp out the door when she felt that the minister was directing his sermon at her. The minister would stop in mid-sentence to watch her make the exit, and this would happen at nearly every service she attended. Afterwards, we would find her sitting in the car, just waiting for us to come out of the church. On the drive home, we would listen to her rant about how awful the minister was and about his terrible sermon. I was secretly happy on the Sundays that she chose to stay home and not attend service, though I would also feel guilty for thinking such thoughts. It was a very small church, and everyone took notice of her exits as she would pop up out of her seat with a heated look on her face and make a quick exit. I would feel like sliding right under the pew in embarrassment. My sister May would just give me a glance, as if to say, here we go again. The first few times that it happened, my father followed behind her. After about the third time, though, he just let her go and he remained in his seat. The worst moments were during the holidays, when she seemed to get most irritated about the minister's sermons. I remember being only thirteen and wondering what it was that made her so disturbed with him. The minister would graciously shake our hands at the end of the sermon, however, as though nothing had happened. I wondered what he thought about my mother's behavior, and if he knew about her disease, and I also questioned what other members of the congregation knew about my mother or if they secretly talked behind our backs about her strange and dramatic exits out of the church. On several occasions, a fellow church goer would try to bait me with a question about her, but I would just smile and shrug my shoulders, and say, "I don't know."

Holidays were almost always filled with tension revolving around her mood swings and irrational behavior. She sometimes did not want to get out of bed, or she would be in a really foul mood if she did. This would place a damper on any joy or excitement surrounding the season.

I believe the minister in our church knew about her illness because he made regular visits to our home to visit with my mother. My sister and I would sometimes be at home during these visits, and we would witness a little bit of her interaction with him before escaping outside or to another part of the house. Sometimes my mother would tell us not to hang around during those visits, warning us off prior to his arrival. I believe that she may have had a crush on him, judging by her very obvious tone of voice and laughter. I had witnessed this same behavior when other men had flirted with her. I'm not so sure that the minister was flirting with her, however.

My mother could be very sweet and a lot of fun when she was in a good mood, though. She had a quick wit and her laugh could be contagious. During the moments when I saw her laugh, it was as though she was just like any other normal mom, and she seemed to enjoy the minister's visits despite her irritation on Sundays in regards to his sermons. I noticed that her face would turn red, and she had a certain tone to her laughter when he was around. After the minister made his departure, she would be in a good mood and it would last for a few days afterward. I was captivated by her change in mood, and questioned her as to what their discussion had been about. Her response was one that kept her mystery alive, as she did not want to reveal anything about their discussion.

I am positive that my mother never cheated on my father in a physical way, but I truly wondered what her thoughts were about our minister. I wondered what he said that so intrigued her, and why her attitude changed so drastically during his visits. I also wondered how someone's thoughts about how they felt about someone could change so drastically from moment to moment. I was bewitched by the complexity of her personality, and quite often found her difficult to understand.

Members of our church, neighbors, and family friends probably also found her to be a curiosity. As an outsider looking in, they may have wondered about her, but not been quite sure of the nature of her problem. When her disappearance came about, though, the state of my mother was no longer wrapped in secrecy.

Once the news of her most recent disappearance was on the local news media, it was out in the open and others were now aware of "her condition". It was almost a game changer for me, because prior to this I had worried that people would treat me differently, as though I was "the apple that did not fall far from the tree". My sister and I had had concerns that we would have the same disease one day, and we'd made a pact "that we would take care of each other" no matter what; that pact even included dignity issues, such as keeping each other's faces well groomed. We would often say out loud to each other that we hoped that neither one of us would end up like her, and that if we did we would tell each other that our behavior was like that of our mother. Out thinking was that a comment like that would immediately snap us out of any illness that might have gotten to us.

Nobody ever told me directly that I was just like my mother, but my family doctor did tell me one time during a visit, "You know how your mother is." Whether he was alluding to the fact that I could be like her or was just giving me a scare to take care of my own mental health, I'm not sure. I never did figure out what he was trying to tell me. Looking back, I think that he may have wondered how her condition affected me. Maybe he threw that out to me as a gauge of my response, knowing I was so used to bottling up my concerns in regards to my mother.

Our family physician was wonderful in regards to the care of both my parents and myself. He was my family physician for many years, prior to my moving from the area. To this day, he still remains as my mother's family physician. Early in life, I was shy and didn't talk much about my mother or my situation at home in regards to her behavior. Acquaintances would ask about her and I didn't divulge much information at all about her condition. I was always very good about holding my emotions inside in my younger years. During this period of time, when she disappeared, I was not comfortable talking about it to anyone... and really, I just wanted to avoid any outside discussions. I harbored a lot of my feelings about my mother inside my own mind, as they were so confusing.

I had a part-time summer job at a local dairy mart during my mother's disappearance. My fellow employees who were now aware of her condition would ask me about her while we were waiting for her to resurface; every day, they would kindly ask me if there was any word about her return. I appreciated their concern, but didn't satisfy their curiosity regarding the details about my daily life with her. My sister and I would make fun at times about her peculiarities or about a particular situation, and would sometimes include other relatives in our silliness, but we were pretty protective when it came to anyone else.

During the several weeks of waiting for any word in regards to the whereabouts of my mother, I tried my best to live my life as normally as possible. I did all of the duties of maintaining the household, as well as working at the dairy mart. I was home alone with my father and I tried my best to keep him well fed and taken care of. I kept myself very occupied partly so as to not dwell on thoughts about my mother. I wondered how she could just disappear and not tell anyone, and I also wondered about her welfare, and where she could possibly have gone. Once again, I wondered if I would ever see her again and why she'd left in the first place.

Our concerns finally came to an end when a chambermaid at a hotel twenty miles away from our home saw her picture on television and called the sheriff. That phone call resulted in her admittance to the mental ward for a few weeks afterwards. All over again, the doctors needed to get her medication under control. She had stopped taking her medications, and her thoughts had been that my father harbored intentions of killing her. Her paranoia had sent her into a delusional state that had no basis in fact.

Visits to the mental ward were uncomfortable in many respects. We would usually stay away for the first week and give the team of workers an opportunity to get her medications regulated. On the few times where we made a visit soon after her admittance, my mother would be sulking and distant. Talking was usually not very interactive, as hard as we would try to make conversation, as she would be very quiet. I was sure it was a result of the drugs.

My sister and I would be highly observant of the other residents as they were acting out their various symptoms of their diseases. It was sometimes difficult to pay attention to my mother, in fact, as we were often distracted by some display of unusual behavior that would catch our attention. It appeared that she was not very interested in talking with us anyway, as she would just sit and stare at us. It was very odd to see our beautiful and well-groomed mother in nice clothes, there and sitting amongst the other patients who had food-soiled clothes and could care less about how they looked or behaved around strangers. I felt sorry that she had to be confined to a residence that she shared with such untidy habits, and with no one to make decent conversation with. I always hoped that her stay would be short and that she'd return home as soon as possible.

The ward keeping her was attached to a local hospital, and it was fairly new and clean – but it was always an interesting experience, as well. Upon leaving her behind, I always wondered what happened in there after we left. I wouldn't cry in front of her, but I would sometimes cry myself to sleep when thinking about her difficulties. These visits always made a statement to me about the reality that she was living in, and it was not the one that I was familiar with, nor one that I wanted as my own.

The stays in the mental ward could last for several weeks or more depending on her progress. She always returned home in a more stabilized condition, though. Sometimes, it was very evident that she had been highly medicated, as she appeared to be almost lacking in any emotion. She would sit on the sofa and watch television for most of the day, with the same distant look on her face that she'd worn during our visits. I was happy to have her home, but it was always an adjustment, as to how she was going to interact with us upon her return. Each time, I would hope that it would be her last visit, and that they could work out her medications so that she could have a normal life. Her complaints about the medications were that they made her feel funny, that they made her throat dry, that she did not need them, and that there was nothing wrong with her. Legally, we couldn't make her take the medications, and we could only keep an eye on them to see if she was taking them. I know that the doctors she was working with were constantly making adjustments and changes to the types of medications that she was taking, as the unpredictability surrounding her reactions to the medication was sometimes just as mysterious as the disease itself.

When I was in my mid-thirties, I had to take some time away from work to attend a hearing where my mother had been summoned to appear before the court. I was no longer living at home and my father had great concerns in regards to her well-being. He was not able to convince her to take her medications or to commit herself to the mental ward. Once again, she had stopped taking her medications and her strange behavior had gotten out of hand.

My mother's paranoia had become more evident than in previous years. She'd been talking constantly about my father's intentions of getting rid of her. We were fearful that she would hurt herself or my father but, without her attempting either act, we were unable to have her committed. We asked her to commit herself, but she wanted no part of that, as she felt that she was fine. In the past, she had agreed to being committed after some convincing or some event would lead to her admittance. This particular time, though, the more that my father attempted to have her commit herself, the more she felt that he was plotting against her. More and more, he was aware that something was brewing that was not healthy, and was concerned for her safety as well as his own. She had already applied for a gun permit previously and he didn't want her to own a firearm. He just wasn't totally sure of what she was capable of, because she had surprised him so many times. He finally came to the conclusion that it was better to be proactive in regards to her care, rather than to wait till something happened that would cause her to be admitted.

In the past, he had always been hesitant to do anything about her issue unless it became an acute problem. He seemed fine to let things go for a period of time before addressing the issue and, as a result, things could get out of hand. I think his past experiences had finally led him to believe that he needed to do something to head this one off before anything drastic happened. So, after many discussions with her psychiatrist, the only alternative that my father had was to have her served with a subpoena to appear before the court.

Every family member was asked to attend the court hearing in order to testify in regards to her behavior. In conjunction with the psychiatrist, my father planned the day of her summons with much thought. He arranged for my sister and I to wait in our car several miles away from our family home. Once the sheriff's car that contained my mother passed us by, we were then to fall in behind the car and follow it to the hearing. My sister and I waited with much nervousness and anxiety for the sheriff's car to drive up the mountain road which we had travelled. We'd waited in the parking lot of a camp that was located not far from our country home.

Over all of the years of her illness, we'd never had to testify about her behavior, and so this was something new for all of us. We were clueless as to what the judge would ask us about our mother, and yet we would have to testify right in front of her. She had just been apprehended by a sheriff, and I was sure she would not be in a good mood.

Once my sister and I joined our brothers and father at the hearing, we entered the room together. The room was attached to the mental ward and was not an actual courtroom, as I had imagined. Once the hearing started, much to our relief, the judge asked my mother one or two questions, based on which he got the needed responses to have her committed. We were all released from the duty of having to testify against her in order to have her placed in the mental ward. Her psychiatrist was present, though, and he'd offered testimony in regards to her condition. It was a stressful day for our family and a relief for us to know that she would once again receive the care that she so badly needed, however unfortunate it was that we'd had to go through the legal system to have her placed where she needed to be in order to retain her reality.

This was the last time that my father had to be involved in

getting this type of help for my mother. Not long after the hearing, my mother's psychiatrist retired and she was assigned to a new psychiatrist. The new psychiatrist was a younger woman, and she seemed to take a new approach in helping my parents to deal with her disease. My father accompanied my mother to her appointments on a regular basis and, as a result, it seemed to make her disease more manageable. Previously, my father had rarely visited with her psychiatrist, but the new doctor wanted him to be more involved. Her approach was successful, thank goodness, as it seemed to make a difference. I know that her medications were changed, and that she took them on a regular basis. It was not the end of the troubles that my father would have in dealing with her illness, but it was the last time he would have to visit the mental ward. Later on in life, though, my sister and I would become more responsible for her care and we would make a few more of those types of visits.

In thinking back about my relationship with my mother, I've learned not to have any expectations of my mother showing any outpouring of emotion for anyone. The medications that she took kept her highly altered, and sometimes her face would reflect that state of mind. Early on, I learned that any emotional problems that she displayed were related to her disease, and that they were something that she seemed to have no control over. Her disease was very difficult for other people to understand. In observing physical diseases such as cancer, the signs are utterly visible, and there can be an immediate awareness that someone is ill. With mental illness, the symptoms are not so visible, and there may be little or no awareness that someone has such a disease; knowledge of it can sometimes be a surprise that comes out of nowhere, just as living with my mother and her changes was so often a surprise to be dealt with. There were times when my mother didn't remember that she'd reacted to a particular situation in a certain way, and would deny that she'd ever behaved that way when questioned. Many times, I would become very disgusted with her and the way that she would manipulate other people, including myself. Yet, it was something we all learned to live with.

I love my mother very much, but I have realized that she has a disease and that part of the disease is her self-absorbed behavior. The sad realization is that, over her entire life, she has had no concern for anybody but herself. And unfortunately, my father – in his very loving way – spent his entire married life caring for her, with little or no expectations in return.

My Father

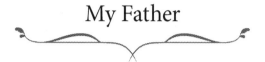

You may wonder what kind of person spends their entire life caring for someone with such dedication. The man who I called my father was such a person. He loved my mother and was committed to her care for the entirety of his life. I have always recognized that my father was a special individual, in that he had a high level of integrity as well as a high level of patience. I admired him and loved him with all of my heart, but at the same time wondered how he could handle all of his responsibilities with such ease. At times, I pondered whether he struggled internally with his responsibilities or his relationship with my mother.

I know from the stories regarding their dating years that my father was immediately smitten with my mother. She was a pretty woman, and they met at local dairy nook in their small town. He was introduced to her through a mutual friend and the relationship got started, and it wasn't long afterward that my father was sent into the Navy. They wrote love letters to each other during his absence, and upon his return he proposed to her. Supposedly, he'd overheard that someone else was going to ask for her hand in marriage and had decided to beat them to it. In fact, my mother had dated someone else while he was away. In a recent discussion I had with my mother, though, she revealed that she was in love with my father even then and that she knew he was in love with her.

I am sure that my father was taken with her beauty, but he was probably also attracted to my mother's good sense of humor. My father loved to joke around and he seemed to be able to make my mother laugh. They had a certain tenderness between them that would come out on Sundays when they would work in the kitchen together, preparing our dinner. It was in those moments when I could see how much my father did love my mother, by his gentle touches on her arm or a private joke that they would share. His attitude towards her was always one of kindness, and he played a dual role in not only caring about her, but caring for her.

My father had a similar role in my life, acting not only as my father but in many cases playing the role of my mother. He was the one who got May and I out of bed every morning to make sure that we had a nice breakfast before going off to school. I still have a vision of him tapping the toaster with his knife and humming a happy tune out loud as he waited for the toast to pop. At six o'clock in the morning, he could be quite cheerful, and I admit it could be a bit annoying when one was feeling sleep deprived. If I'd only known at the time that, later in life, I would cherish such a moment. I would give anything to go back in time and to be able to hear him sing and tap the toaster once again. You see, he was always cheerful and trying hard to joke with me as I arrived at the morning kitchen table, still feeling tired after a full night of rest.

My father always carried an even temperament that contrasted with my mother's erratic mood. I may not have always known what he was thinking, but it was a rare moment when I saw him get angry or annoyed with anyone. He had the patience of a saint, and people often referred to him as being one. I would guess that it had something to do with his tolerating the antics of my mother. The times when my parents did have words with each other, they never got out of control. They always managed to keep their composure in front of us. My father only needed to give me his "special look" for me to know that I'd made a breach in judgement. It was his way of keeping us in check. I got reprimanded a few times in response to my mother's desire to have me do the evening dishes, especially. I would sometimes stall in front of the television set or argue with May as to whose turn it was to actually pick up and wash the dishes. I always felt as though May was my father's favorite because it seemed at the time as though

I was constantly being made to be the responsible one for anything that was out of line.

The only real telltale sign that he could be the least bit annoyed was the smoke that would roll out of the pipe that he smoked. For many years, our home and car smelled like crisp roasted apples from his tobacco. If he became the least bit irritated, he would bite his teeth down on his pipe and his face would flow into a thoughtful look. The speed of the smoke coming out of his pipe would triple its pace. Later in life, he even had to have his false teeth replaced because he had bored a hole in them where he gripped his pipe with his front teeth. My sister and I found it to be humorous, as he showed us the remnants of his false teeth. He had to have a whole new set of teeth made as a result. I'm sure that was a consequence of the constant stress of clenching his teeth.

Even though I have never enjoyed the smell of cigarette smoke, I found his pipe smoke to be comforting. After my father was gone, I kept his favorite pipe and would sometimes take a whiff just to be reminded of his odor.

My father spent his entire life not only caring for our family, but caring for other people, as well. His profession was that of being a caretaker for a private country club located in a rural town in Pennsylvania. We grew up in a coal mining community, but lived amongst the more monetarily well-to-do because of my father's profession. Our home was situated on a beautiful golf course beside a small lake and outdoor swimming pool. In the summertime, the community came to life with executives arriving from the city to enjoy their summer homes and all of the amenities. We were fortunate to have access to the golf course, swimming pool, and tennis court that the picturesque country club contained within its fenced in property. The winter could be desolate, though it reminded me of a picture-perfect postcard from some remote town in Switzerland because of the way that it was nestled amongst the snowcapped Laurel mountains. In the wintertime, it was so quiet that the only sound was often that of the snow falling to the ground.

During both seasons, my father worked hard to keep the extensive property perfectly groomed and manicured. He had a small crew of workers that helped him to be responsible for the twenty-two vacation homes located on the grounds. When the owners were absent, he made sure that everything was safe and secure. He would typically get phone calls at all times of the day and night to tend to their needs, and he spent many weekends and long evenings repairing golf carts that had broken down, evaluating and repairing plumbing problems, watering the greens, and taking care of other immediate problems that would arise.

Situated at the peak of the property sits a large white clubhouse that still to this day looks like Mount Vernon. Standing and looking out from its lengthy gray porch, one witnesses a beautiful view of the quiet lake with a rustic, stone dam below it. During the summer months, this clubhouse buzzed with activity as its members enjoyed all three meals in the spacious wood floored dining room. Every summer, a talented chef was hired and brought on board with his temporary staff to fulfill the needs of all of the hungry guests.

The beautiful century-old clubhouse had its share of problems during the height of the season and my father was constantly tending to all types of issues related to the care of such a huge building. The members of the club, though, appreciated the many talents that my father possessed in addressing all of their needs, as well as the various challenges offered up by the property. Simply, he loved his job and took great pride in his work. They couldn't have hired a more kind-hearted man to provide them with the services that they required, and they generally realized it. In appreciation, some of the club members would individually reward him with extra cash for his good services. Of course, in any situation, there are always a few folks who you can never make happy, no matter what you do. I am sure he dealt with a few of those types, but he would never have made it known even if he did feel any dissatisfaction.

When he wasn't directly helping out members of the club, my father loved to tinker in the club workshop, and he worked tirelessly on any repair project that needed to be taken care of. My father was a very creative man, and could fix almost anything that was broken;

if he did not have what he needed, he would conjure something up to repair it! Work was simpler than home, I imagine, because of this – because unfortunately for my father, the one thing that he could not repair was my mother. As you know by now, my mother was not an easy person to live with, and as hard as he tried, he could not fix her. Yet, though he knew about my mother's blemish, he loved her deeply regardless. We were never allowed to say anything negative about my mother or he would correct us with a reminder of, "That is your mother that you are talking about." My father was great at being a father, as well as a mother, in constantly reminding us of all of our p's and q's, especially when it came to our mother. He wanted his daughters to be respectful of not only our mother, but everyone else also. He had great morals and wanted us to follow in these same footsteps. Not only was my father a wonderful teacher in this respect, but he was also a mentor to us in organization and when it came to achieving our goals.

It was my father who made sure that my sister and I got to all of our necessary medical appointments and afterschool activities. He attended all of our sporting events, and was very proud of us and our accomplishments. Sometimes he would politely brag to others about our achievements, and I would occasionally even feel embarrassed about the attention he called to how well we were doing with a particular activity or with our school grades. He'd never completed high school himself, so it was important to him that we got a good education and did well in school. Neither of my parents completed high school, actually, because of their premature adult duties and the economically poor times that they grew up in. Thankfully, they were both blessed with being able to figure things out for themselves without much guidance from anyone. They seemed to manage in the world solely on their own, and without much socialization with other couples outside of the family circle.

My mother's illness made it difficult for them keep friends to socialize with on a regular basis, truth be told. If they did start a relationship with another couple, it would ultimately be destroyed as a result of my mother's paranoid tendencies. She would end up accusing anyone who they socialized with of having "wronged" her in some way.

At one time, my parents took up square dancing at the local community center and became friends with a few of the other couples who they interacted with. My mother seemed to be enjoying herself and she even made her own square dancing dresses, and made my father matching shirts. They looked forward to those evenings when they would go out dancing. Unfortunately, it seemed that nearly as soon as they became acquainted with some of the other couples, they became aware of her problem. The relationships did not last long because they found it too difficult to maintain the friendships, despite my father's best efforts. Most of the time, they would stay in touch – but they would be excluded from being invited to a number of parties and events.

I would feel bad for my father, as he was so very pleasant to be around and people seemed to really enjoy his company. He had a wonderful sense of humor and could find the joy in almost any activity.

My parents did remain close with their brothers and sisters despite the fact that my mother attempted to ruin those ties, as well. She didn't even speak to the wife of one of my father's brothers for a long period of time because she accused her of checking our house for dust! I found out later that my father had made early morning visits to their home without my mother, just to keep the relationship intact.

My own relationship with my father early in life was a bit strained due to my mother portraying him as the heavy-handed one. My mother would always be telling us to "Wait until your father gets home." When he'd arrive home from work, he was usually tired and would just reinforce that it was time to do chores, and that any talking back to our mother was forbidden. My father never laid a hand on us, but he always told us to follow her instructions. My mother, though, slapped my mouth once or twice for talking back to her.

I was in the third grade when we moved to our home at the country club, and that's when the dual relationship became more noticeable. My mother seemed to shrink into the background and my relationship with my father became more apparent. May and I spent more time outdoors playing on the grounds and helping our father with some of his activities, and we got to be known at the club as our father's helpers. My father taught me how to play golf and arranged for my sister and I to have tennis and piano lessons. During the summer, we played outside till the sun set every night, and we would have to be called for several times to get us inside. And in the winter, we would sled down the golf course hills till we were so cold that we could barely move!

It was after our move to the country club that I became friendly with a few of the neighbor boys who I met on our school bus. They came to our yard to play with me and I became irritated with my father for chasing them away. At that time, I didn't understand his concerns about his daughter playing with boys, and so I couldn't understand his actions. I became a little bit resentful at that point, and started to withdraw into my own little shell as a result. I much preferred to have boys as friends than girls, as it was easier for me to relate to them since I enjoyed playing football and riding my bicycle full speed down any embankment that I could find. For some reason, I didn't get much enjoyment from the dolls that I owned at the time.

By the time I was in the seventh grade, I started to mature into a woman and I became quite self-conscious about the changes that had started to take place in my body. My insecurities about my own sexuality changed my relationship with my father. Prior to these changes, I'd given both my mother and father a kiss goodnight and a hug before going to bed every night, it being a ritual of ours as they sat in the living room watching television. As I became aware of my bodily changes, though, I suddenly felt bashful about giving my father a hug and kiss. It may, in retrospect, be that I was becoming a woman, and I felt awkward with my own sexuality. I know that I hurt his feelings when those sweet hugs and kisses stopped, and I am sure he wondered why – hopefully, he understood. It was nothing that my father had done, and only an effect of my own uncomfortable feelings. Those hugs and kisses returned when I graduated from high school and went off to college. It was as though, I suppose, his teenage daughter left for a while and then came back later.

My sweet father also suffered through some uncomfortable moments of not knowing how to relate to me. He tried so hard to talk with me while riding alone with me in the car, and I just would not open up to him in spite of his efforts. I can remember several very strained car rides where I couldn't wait to get out of the car. The questions that he asked were simple questions about school and the activities in which I was involved, and nothing over invasive, but despite everything that he had done for me I was afraid of sharing too much information with him. When I wouldn't give him anything to work with, he would sing or hum to himself as he drove us to our destinations. Our car rides changed later on to being full of delightful chatter when he'd pick me up from college to bring me home for a weekend visit or summer break. I'd look forward to his arrival then, and our long drives home together would give us time to talk alone. Of course, my mother would rarely ride along with him to pick me up or take me back to school.

As unpredictable as my mother could be, though, my father was the opposite. He was a very dependable man and never disappointed me in regards to being trustworthy. If he told me that he would be somewhere at a certain time, I could always count on him to arrive at least five minutes early. I'm grateful that I had such a strong father figure who looked after me with such care and concern.

A few times in my life, I ended up in the hospital for knee surgeries, wisdom teeth removal, and another malady that caused me to become deathly ill. It was my father who I could count on to take me to the hospital or arrive to meet with the doctors in regards to the various situations. He was also the one who encouraged me to go to college and who helped me to decide the course of study that I would follow. I was the only child to attend college and, despite my parents' tight budget, he made sure that I got all the grants and loans that I needed to see me through. I worked during the summers to pay for my schooling and he always made sure that I had the family vehicle available to get me to work and back. If he needed the car on any particular day, he would drop me off and then pick me up at the end of my shift. He was a selfless man, in that he was always thinking about the needs of his family instead of himself. He wasn't remotely materialistic, and the only thing that he spent money on for himself was golfing and those vacations to Florida during the winter months when it was off-season.

The golf weekends and trips to Florida took place when May and I were in high school and continued on an annual basis until the last year of his life. He didn't tolerate the cold very well, and found the Pennsylvania winters to be cold and depressing. The extra money that he received from his extra duties was put aside for their two months in Florida; my parents would usually leave for Florida right after Christmas and come back at the end of February. There was not as much constructive work to do in the winter months in the way of maintaining the club, except for plowing the roads, making sure everyone had heat and that the water pipes didn't burst, and doing maintenance on the machinery used in the summertime. He was able to leave things in the hands of another employee for that short period of time. I know that he cherished his time away, and he spent a lot of the time golfing with my mother during those vacations. He also worked on creative projects such as putting photos in picture albums, designing mailboxes, and writing letters to friends and acquaintances. In fact, my father kept in touch with me during my college years by writing me letters.

During my college years, I received a letter every week from my father, along with a twenty- dollar bill and a humorous story or a joke. I looked forward to those letters that were filled with news from home and which always had a positive feel to them. When he'd been in grade school, he'd received an award for his penmanship, and his handwriting was absolutely beautiful. I would sometimes get packages filled with some of my favorite treats and, on April Fool's day, I could expect an empty package with a simple note that said, "April Fools." Every year, I swore that I was not going to open that particular package – but my curiosity always got the best of me. I have kept most of those letters in an old shoebox filed away in the closet, as I am just not ready to part with them; that's how much they meant to me over the years.

With his favorite holiday being Halloween, I also have lots of photos of the various hand-designed costumes that he would create. Our front yard would be decorated with some interesting characters that would make me laugh hilariously or, alternately, shrink in embarrassment. He would stuff some old clothes with dried leaves to make odd-looking persons, complete with masked faces, sometimes placing them on a bicycle or rocking horse in the yard or on the front porch steps. They'd usually be wearing some sort of hat and have an arm raised in the air to look like it was waving to passerby. I always wondered what they had to do with Halloween, but it would nonetheless make me laugh as I sidestepped their placements about the yard.

As another outlet for his creativity, he took to designing and creating unusual mailboxes. His best creation was a three-foot diameter golf ball mailbox that was complete with dimples and which sat on a tee carved out of a log. That monster of a mailbox took him two years to design and build, and it was recognized in a magazine called *Country Creations*. Some of the local teenagers found it to be a challenge to dismantle and roll the large ball down the road on a regular basis. It was a frustrating occurrence to my father, but that mailbox always got remounted and put back in its rightful place at the end of our walkway. He'd usually give such mailboxes to family members or as a special gift to someone else. A few of the readers of that magazine issue requested he make them a golf ball mailbox. I don't think that they realized the enormity of the project. He wrote down the instructions for how they could make it themselves and sent those along to them instead.

Every year, a major Easter egg hunt took place in our family kitchen, set up for just my sister and I to participate. Most families held these type of activities in their backyard, but he enjoyed hiding the eggs amongst pots and pans. We enjoyed the Easter egg hunt until we were in our late twenties, and then we received a reprieve because my sister had two sons to take our place. I could see the disappointment on my father's face when we finally decided that we were too old for such games. The eggs were hidden so well that he sometimes couldn't remember where he'd hid them. But despite the fact that my mother was generally in a strange mood for the holidays, he always made them fun. I wondered how he could be so happy at times while my mother was in one of her moods, and sometimes even missing from holiday celebrations due to her being in an institution.

Shortly after my mother was diagnosed with her illness, a major change in my father's sleeping arrangements took place. It was during the summer school break of my high school freshman year that my mother asked my sister and I to help move our father's dresser from their bedroom. May and I refused to help, so she took it upon herself to push his dresser across the long upstairs hallway and into a spare bedroom. May and I didn't want to have anything to do with that move. When we questioned her about putting our father into another room, she accused him of having an affair with one of the club members. I tried hard to imagine that situation, and just couldn't bring it to fruition in my own mind. My father worked out in nature on a daily basis, and he was usually dressed in some worn and somewhat dirty work clothes with work boots, and he was catering to some very well-dressed women in their nicely cleaned and pressed versions of sporty golf and tennis attire. My father was attractive and nice, but I couldn't imagine that one of the club ladies I'd seen would have any interest in pursuing my father or that he'd have any interest in them. It was always obvious that he was dedicated to my mother in spite of all the problems or my mother challenging him on the subject, but though my father endured a lot from my mother, he truly loved her. I didn't have any doubt in my mind about the thoughts of my father. Of course, when he was dressed for church in his sports jacket and tie or other casual wear, he was quite impressive. Those types of clothes only came out for special occasions or if he was going somewhere that he needed to be dressed up. Regardless, I knew how he felt about my mother.

On the day when she moved my father out of the bedroom, I took it upon myself to go hunt my father down and inform him of his new sleeping arrangements. I walked out onto the course to find him with a pitcher of lemonade and a snack in hand, to prepare him with the news. He took the news with his usual calm demeanor, but I did notice the telltale, heavy roll of smoke come out of the pipe he was smoking at the time. I wondered what was going to happen upon his arrival home.

My parents usually kept their personal discussions behind closed doors, and so we children weren't privy to their concerns or disagreements, and this matter was no exception. I know that my father spent the next few years in that spare bedroom, and I wondered how he lived with a wife who did not sleep with him. It wasn't until I left for the Jersey Shore that he moved back into her bedroom. The only reason that it occurred at that time was as a result of my sister, her husband, and their new baby who were moving into our family home for the summer, and so they needed to utilize that room. I'm positive that my father was happy to be back in her bedroom when the time did come, and he seemed to be a happier person as a result.

In my senior year of high school, especially, I found myself feeling sorry for my father – as I could see a change in his morale. My mother was being extremely difficult with all of the members of her family at the time, and we could sometimes hear noisy discussions taking place in another room behind closed doors. I wondered to myself how they were still married and why he had not filed for a divorce. I told myself that I would not have put up with her behavior, and that I wouldn't stay with a spouse who acted in such a manner. I was thinking about my future already, and I wasn't imagining a marriage to be like that of my parents. I went to school feeling depressed about their situation because I knew that, at that time, they were not a very happy couple. I wondered why he would not just leave her, and then I thought about the future she would have without him. I felt that my mother was very fortunate to have married a man like my father then, as most men would not have lasted long in such a situation.

They somehow muddled through their marriage for the next few years, though. Eventually, my father and I did sometimes have serious conversations about their relationship. I had wondered what happened when they went on vacation to Florida, and if they slept together at that time and how they got along together. Later on, when I was an adult, my father shared with me that they occasionally had relations during those times away. I felt at the times that my father really just needed to talk with someone about his situation, and I could see his heartbreak on his face. To close out those conversations, he would think of something funny to take away the heaviness and we would laugh together. He never wanted me or any of his children to carry the burden of any of his problems with our mother. I knew even when I was young that the problems he carried as a result of my mother's illness would surely take a toll on his physical health, and eventually the problems made their appearance.

During the summer of my senior year of high school, he had a bleeding ulcer that became a life and death situation – as he waited until it became an emergency to address it. That evening at the dinner table, he didn't eat his dinner and he instead complained of not feeling well. He indicated that he had some pain, and an hour later he was wall-papering the same hallway that his dresser had passed through when he was overcome with even more intense pain. I don't know why he didn't rest after dinner and went ahead with the chore at hand. I don't recall if it was at my mother's insistence, but I remember being concerned about him since I knew that he didn't feel well.

Fortunately, one of the club members who was a physician came to our home to assess the situation, and he called for an ambulance. My father was rushed to the hospital and then immediately into the operating room, where they cut his vagus nerve to stop the bleeding. My mother seemed to have no concern for his well-being at all, and had to put on makeup and change clothes before she would leave the house for the hospital. My sister and I had to wait patiently as she prepped herself in order to make the forty-five-minute ride. I was disgusted with her lack of emotion and concern for the situation, and with her once again self-centered attitude as my father nearly died.

Two years later, he passed out while working on the golf course and I was called to come home from college, as he'd had a major TIA. He was in intensive care at the age of fifty-five and they had great concern for him, as they were not sure what had precipitated such an event. He recovered, though, and returned to work several weeks later without any seemingly lasting physical problems, but he was warned to take it easy. At the time, it was believed that his illness was a result of all the hard work that he did at the club.

Even as my father worked hard at the club, after my sister and I were gone from the house, my mother also relied on my father to do the chores that we had once taken care of. She was physically capable of doing the housework and the chores, but she was just too lazy. My mother was very good at manipulating people to do things for her, and my father was now the target. Being the easy-going guy that he was, he would oblige her in order to avoid any domestic squabbles that might occur as a result of any pushback. Simply, he was very much a man who loved peace amongst his family members, and he often went above and beyond to make sure that everyone was happy – regardless of his own mental or physical well-being.

Starting in my late twenties, on my visits to my parents' home for a long weekend, I almost always would see my father retire early in the evening to his favorite chair, where he would fall fast asleep. Approximately around 11 p.m., he would retire to his bedroom and I would then hear his radio turn on, and there he would listen to a talk show until he fell back to sleep. He was up at the crack of dawn every day of the week and was usually out the door by 7:30 every morning. Once a week, he would sit at the kitchen table to pay bills and write notes to friends and acquaintances. I knew that he was not only physically exhausted from all of his duties, but mentally exhausted, as well. I could see that my father – who always seemed calm, energetic, and positive – was slowly being worn down by my mother's requests.

The most enjoyment that my father found in life seemed to be on the golf course. We played as a family in the dusk of the day after all of the club members returned to their private homes and prepared for dinner. At that time of the day, we had the entire golf course to ourselves and could play until darkness set in. My father and I had many memorable moments on the golf course, and we often played by ourselves when I was in my late twenties and early thirties. I would come home to spend time with him on the weekends, and that would invariably include several rounds of golf. In the fall of the year, when the club was closed, we would travel to other golf courses to be challenged by something new and different. It was during those times when I really enjoyed being with both of my parents. My mother would act up during these times, as well, but it was to be expected. Quite often, my brother Martin would also join us and we would have a lot of laughs together.

On my weekend visits home, my father would routinely buy some Oreo cookies for us to share. It was our special time together, when we would sit and talk about life in general and eat our cookies as we dunked them in a big glass of milk. He would quietly listen as I would tell him about both my joys and concerns, and he would make suggestions as to how I might handle certain situations with love and integrity. He was also the one who I called on a nightly basis during the week to talk to about my day. I know that sometimes he was exhausted not only by his day but by my endless chatter on the other end of the line, but he always had the time to listen and reassure me about any lack of self-confidence that I might have been experiencing. The greatest lesson that he taught me was to "Pull your own wagon" in life, and, most importantly, to "be happy."

My greatest sadness and the greatest loss in my life was that of my father. I was forty years old at the time of his passing, and my life was in a flux of change. I had just opened my own art gallery when I got the call that my father had suffered a major stroke. He along with my mother had just attended the grand opening of my business a week prior to the call. It was the fall of 1998, and I had been working hard to get my store built and opened. Earlier, that spring, I had been out to Chicago to a trade school for several months to learn the business. Thus, I'd been busy, and not around to spend time with him so much as I would have liked.

I had spent the summer fully focused on learning how to operate and run my own business, my life had become a whirlwind of new responsibilities, and I had enveloped myself in my own world of building out my store in preparation. My parents had made several surprise trips to my shop in Pittsburgh to visit with me, though. I'm ashamed to say that, during that time, I was so involved with what I was doing that I could barely pull myself away to eat lunch with them. They were making special hour-long trips to see me, and I wasn't giving them the respect that they so deserved. My visits to their home had slowed down for other reasons also by then, as I was spending weekends with my husband at our second home on the lake. I don't recall that I had played one game of golf with my father that spring or summer. It was such a busy time in my life that time just slipped by, and when I think back on it, I realize I was quite oblivious to what was happening with my own father and mother. I have to confess that I was pretty self-absorbed and was quite anxious about my new adventure. I was neglecting those who I loved as a result, as I was planning for my future success. I'm regretful of my actions, as my father had always made time for me, and now that he needed to have time with me I wasn't available.

I didn't realize it at the grand opening of my business, but my life was about to change forever. The event of my father's stroke was something that I could never have prepared for in a million years.

The last time that I spoke to him was on the day of my grand opening event. Afterward, I called on the telephone and I kept missing him, as he wasn't available to speak. It was summertime, and he was outdoors enjoying nature. Even so late as on the morning of his stroke, I had attempted to call my father, and my mother wouldn't fetch him because, once again, he was outside. It wasn't long after that call home that I received the most devastating news of my life. My brother Martin called to say that our father was being taken to a local hospital, and that I needed to get there as soon as possible if I wanted to see him again.

As you can imagine, I was shocked by the news, and I dropped what I was doing to rush to his side. It was the fastest forty-five-minute car ride that I have ever taken. My mind was rushing and my mouth was praying for the stroke not to be fatal. Upon my arrival, my father was barely conscious as I rushed to his side to tell him how much I loved him, and to beg him to please fight to stay alive. The small local hospital where he arrived didn't have the medicine or staff available to care for the brain hemorrhage that he'd suffered, though, so the life flight helicopter was waiting to transport him to a larger hospital, and they had held it up in order for me to see him prior to his departure. He clutched my hands, but wasn't able to say anything as I told him how much I loved him. He waved goodbye to me and the rest of our family members who had arrived to see him – as they loaded him into the helicopter.

Mr. Santini

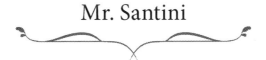

Saying goodbye to my father, whom I loved so very much and cared about, was the most difficult time in my life. My father was the strength that held our family together, and it was his presence in my life that gave me the fortitude to overcome any obstacle which I encountered. Having such a strong father figure in my life, it seems strange even to me that I would develop a relationship with a man who also had authority over me, but that's exactly what happened. I wasn't completely sure of what the attraction was that would make this other figure have such a presence in my life, but had I not encountered him at such an early age, I am sure my life could have taken a very different direction. It was in the eighth grade when I would meet Mr. Santini, who would make a huge impact on my high school years and also leave me with another blemish that would stay with me for years.

I met Mr. Santini on the first day of my eighth-grade science class, as he was my teacher. His appearance was distinct for the area, as his skin always seemed to be tan, he had dishwater blonde hair that was disappearing and a dimpled chin with intense hazel eyes, and he was about my height at the time. I would later tower over him with my five-foot-eight-inch frame. I thought that he was possibly in his late twenties, as he had not been teaching in that school district for very long. He had a nice smile that exemplified the dimple on his chin, but now I remember that he did have some decay on a few of his side teeth – probably from the chewing tobacco that he was so fond of. His hands were spatula-shaped, with fingernails that were unevenly trimmed and sometimes had chewing tobacco underneath them. He always kept a steady supply of lifesavers available to share.

His love of sports was displayed on his classroom walls, as they were filled with pages from the latest sports magazines. He dressed fashionably for the times, wearing leisure suits or a shirt and a nice tie, and he told us how his wife helped him to pick out clothes. He often wore shirts that were the color of purple, which was one of my favorite colors. Loving to read, he always had a best-selling paperback book tucked under his arm as he made his way down the hallway to his next class. He would walk swiftly down the center of the hall in his black-laced coaching shoes, as though he owned the place.

When I first encountered him, I would estimate that he was probably around twenty-eight years old, as he was newly married and they had just had their first child. He shared stories about his wife and his son, who'd been born with some digestive issues. Mr. Santini had quite a commute every morning, which he made with another teacher who worked in the school system. They were both football coaches for the junior and senior high school that I attended. I would watch for their arrival from my desk in my homeroom, as I could see the spot where they parked their car in the parking lot. It was almost an obsessive behavior, and one that mirrored the relationship which would develop between myself and Mr. Santini.

I was thirteen years old, young and impressionable, and striving to fit in with my fellow classmates. At the beginning of that school year, I had participated in a demonstration to be able to wear slacks to school. The sit-in took place in the school lobby and I was encouraged by some older teammates on my sports teams to participate. In the effort to support the cause, as I wanted to be able to wear jeans to school, I joined in with the other participants. I wasn't aware of it at the time, but it would cause me some problems with Mr. Santini.

The sit-in was successful and, as a result, we were able to wear slacks to school. Feeling happy about the situation, I immediately took the opportunity to be comfortable in a pair of jeans. The first few days, only a few students arrived wearing slacks, and I was a minority in my classrooms. Relatively little attention was paid to me prior to my arrival in Mr. Santini's class, though. My face turned red with embarrassment with his class, however, as he immediately called attention to my attire and proclaimed his disdain towards ladies wearing slacks to school. He called me to the front of the classroom and then dismissed me to the school office. I quietly and shyly left his classroom and headed to the office, disturbed by what had just taken place. I wondered what type of retribution I was going to receive from the principal of the school. Under the circumstances, I was confused as to what had just taken place – given the recent approval to wear slacks. I had no sooner arrived in the main office than a fellow classmate came to find me – they'd been instructed to retrieve me back to the classroom.

It was after that incident when I started to notice Mr. Santini staring at me as I was doing my schoolwork in his classroom. I would look up from my desk, only to notice him poised with both arms behind his neck, and he would start a stare-down with me. I would look away and look back, and he would still be staring at me intently. It made me feel uncomfortable and I couldn't figure out why he was constantly staring at me and playing such games. I also noticed that, on the occasions when I would wear dresses to school, he seemed to enjoy looking at my legs; and he made complaints on the days that I would wear slacks. I was a very naïve young lady and I didn't understand at that time what his thoughts might have been about.

My mother had not had the discussion about the birds and the bees with me, and I was pretty unaware – even for that time, perhaps. The previous summer, I had gotten my first period and she had embarrassed me by sharing the information with my older brothers. I had argued with her in the seventh grade about permission to start shaving my legs, as my underarms and legs had been covered with black hair, and a fellow classmate had enjoyed making nasty comments about the growth that was taking place. I'd struggled with my mother about starting the shaving process and she'd finally relented to letting me shave. Such an argument was par for the course. Not feeling perfectly manicured had dampened my self-confidence, as I was still sensitive to being inspected by my peers – even a year later. Standing in front of my classmates was one of my least favorite activities, and I was often called upon to do so by Mr. Santini.

One of his favorite classroom activities was to call someone to the front of the classroom to offer a several minute dissertation on a subject of his choice. He called several people to the front of the room on a daily basis, each of them to be tortured by this process. Speaking in front of the class always made my face turn multiple shades of red due to my self-awareness. I despised the exercise, as I was routinely called up to expound on such topics as love, marriage, kindness, etc. He would throw out almost any topic related to love relationships for me to relay my thoughts on, as compared to my peers who would receive science-related topics. The class found this all to be entertaining, and Mr. Santini found it to be quite enjoyable, as well. The last thing that I wanted to do was to stand in front of my peers and be humiliated, but I was too shy to make any complaints, and so I endured the exhibition of my youthful innocence.

Little did I know at the time that that very innocence was going to be tested by Mr. Santini. It was a known fact throughout the school that Mr. Santini had favorite students who he'd identified through his years of teaching, as he'd invite them back to visit, and would bring them into the classroom and introduce them as such.

One day, Mr. Santini pulled myself and another young lady outside of his classroom door to speak with us alone. My first inclination was to wonder what we had done wrong that had inspired him to call us out to speak with him privately. However, to my surprise, the conversation started with him asking us a strange question regarding our thoughts about him. He wanted to know if we thought about him outside of the classroom and after school hours were done.

Carla was the other student who had joined me in the hall and, like me, she was called upon quite frequently to go to the front of the classroom, and to interpret topics similar to the ones that I was given. She was tall and cute, and her dream was to be a psychologist someday. Carla was a cheerleader and was being raised by her mother as a result of a divorce, so even though she was a cheerleader, she didn't seem to fit in with the rest of the students. In her outgoing way, Carla was the first to respond to Mr. Santini's inquiry, and she answered in the affirmative. In response, I also indicated that I had thought about him outside of school. I had thought about him as I would a friend. A natural tangent of thought that you would have as you started to develop a crush on someone. I wondered what he liked to do after school, and what kind of a house he lived in. What the book was that he was currently reading.

A couple of weeks into that fall semester after the office incident and my beginning to wear slacks, I realized that Mr. Santini was starting to pay a lot of attention to me in the classroom. I wondered if he had singled me out as a result of that perceived problem. In our class, he started to engage in all types of discussions regarding various topics that weren't related to earth and space science. Even though he enjoyed embarrassing me in front of my classmates, though, he had a way of questioning me in regards to my hopes, dreams, and thoughts about various subjects. He would stop in the middle of a classroom discussion and direct some specific questions at me. Questions that were personal in regards to what I did after school and on weekends, what my plans were for the future, and what my thoughts were regarding some subject not related to science. He sometimes even asked me what my favorite food was, and what I'd had for dinner the night before. These were questions that he didn't ask other students, but which seemed to be focused on me in some odd way, expressing some extra interest. In my mind, it showed me that he cared about me in some strange way which I could not quite figure out.

Sometimes, he made me to feel as though I was the only person in the room with him, in the way that he would look at me and talk with me. He had a certain combination of intensity and charismatic charm. The truth was that he had become my favorite teacher in a matter of a few weeks, and I had thought about him periodically. I wondered what he did on weekends and what his home was like. At this point in time, my thoughts about him were nothing unusual in comparison to how I thought of my other teachers. Unaware that I was starting to develop a crush on him due to the attention that he was paying me, I only knew that I was starting to look forward to attending his class more other classes – even though I dreaded getting up in front of the class. I was starting to relax and have fun in his class, as compared to some other classes that were not as much fun.

Back to that day in the hall with Carla, though... having Mr. Santini question us in this fashion didn't come as a complete surprise, but his reaction did. He listened carefully to both of our responses, and then told us both that he thought about us and cared about us. I was taken aback when he asked Carla to step back into the classroom and I was left alone with him. It was then that he shared with me that he loved me in the way that a boyfriend would love a girlfriend. The explanation was that he wanted to kiss me in a sexual way, and that included making love to me. I, of course, was shocked by the revelation, as this was something I hadn't begun to think about. At that stage in my life, I'd only had some minor crushes on a few fellow classmates that had amounted to a few stolen kisses. But my reaction to his declaration sent a very hot feeling through my body which ended in a flushed face. I wasn't capable of uttering any words of pronounced love – or any words at all, for that matter. If I felt anything, I was certainly not going to let anyone know about it, and most certainly not a person for whom I felt some sort of attraction. This was an important moment, though, as I was now truly aware that I had some sort of a crush on him, as well.

Mr. Santini continued to tell me that he thought about me constantly, and out of all of the students that he'd ever taught, I was his "number one". He then asked me if I understood the significance of that. I responded that I understood, but my thoughts raced as to why he would be interested in me at my age and what he expected from me. I also found myself wondering how I could be someone's favorite. He told me that this meant that I was his "number one" favorite person out of all of the students that he had ever taught, more than anyone. For many years after that, "number one" would show up in his written cards, his letters, and even my yearbook, as well as through him telling me often that I *was* his "number one".

I left his classroom that day with a feeling of happiness, knowing that someone cared about me in that way. I had grown fond of him as my teacher and now felt as though I was important to someone, and that he cared about me. My mind wondered immediately how I could be someone's favorite, though – especially when they had a wife and a child. I also knew that there was a significant age difference between us, and I asked myself why he would be attracted to someone like me at all. It was as though his acknowledgement of his feelings toward me made it alright for me to have a crush on him, but I wish I could have realized at the time what emotional damage this would cause me in the future.

The rest of my eighth-grade school year, all I thought about was Mr. Santini. He started to pull me out of other classrooms to speak with me in the hallway or during his lunch duty and lunch hour. He told me many times that he preferred my company to that of the other staff members who were his peers and hung out in the teacher's lounge, and he was constantly writing hall passes for me to reenter a classroom that was not his. Sometimes the other teachers weren't happy about my late admittance and would give me a condescending look or make a small comment. One specifically suggested that I needed to tell Mr. Santini that I needed to get to class on time. A few teachers made reference to Mr. Santini in a negative way and looked directly at me when they did so, suggesting that they wouldn't let their own daughter have him as a teacher. Other students took notice of the attention I was receiving in the classroom also, and in the hallway, and started to refer to me as his girlfriend. My peers enjoyed teasing me about my relationship with Mr. Santini, and my eighth-grade yearbook ended up being filled with comments that referred to him.

Prior to the beginning of the summer between my eighth and ninth year of junior high, arrangements were made between myself and Mr. Santini to meet on the country road that ran in front of my home. He gave me a time frame when he would be passing through the area and he asked me to wait for him to come by. I spent the days of our prearranged meetings trying to figure out how I could nonchalantly escape from the house to make myself available for the secret meetings. Sometimes, babysitting or the evening meal would interfere with the time frame when he was expecting me, but I managed to meet him on several occasions, and it was always nothing more than him talking to me through his open car window as he stared at my legs in my summer shorts. He would always end the conversation with, "I would love to do you–know-what with you."

I would always feel guilty after those meetings, because I wasn't accustomed to lying to my parents about my whereabouts – even though nothing physical took place between us. On Sundays in church, I would repent for the thoughts that I was having about him that revolved around physical pleasure, as I knew that it was wrong to be thinking about him in the way that he was suggesting and I had developed guilty feelings as a result. I wondered if I was going to go to hell as a result of my thoughts, but somehow I couldn't stop myself from participating in this type of behavior.

In the fall of the following year, Mr. Santini was my scheduled teacher for my ninth-grade science class and the relationship continued to develop. I started to feel as though he was my boyfriend and, as a result, I had no interest in boys of my own age. I started to watch for him around school and took every opportunity to see him in the hallways. He would stop by the gym to see me in my after-school basketball and volleyball team practices, and I would always be looking for him and enjoying the time spent away from practice to talk with him for even a few minutes. Sometimes he would even attend a few of my games. It always made me nervous to see him in the crowd, and I would somehow not be able to concentrate on what I was supposed to be doing. I would scan the crowd at various school activities, such as pep rallies and football games, until our eyes would meet. It seemed to me that we were always looking for each other outside of the classroom.

In my ninth-grade year, he encouraged me to try out for the cheerleading team, as that would enable me to ride the bus to football games, for which he was the coach. I competed for a cheering position and dropped out just prior to the judging, as the routine that I'd practiced was difficult and I didn't feel confident in myself. I wasn't sure enough of my ability to make the team because of my shyness, and my feelings of not fitting in with the other girls. I'd also had a terrible time in getting someone to show me the cheers and the routine that needed to be learned. Mr. Santini had finally asked one of the older girls to teach me and to help me with the routine, as I'd shared with him that I didn't know the routines or the cheers and that I needed someone to help me.

My father had also impressed upon me that the cost of the shoes and uniforms would be tight on his budget. He had a very supportive nature, but he wasn't encouraging me to become a cheerleader, and that certainly had some effect. I couldn't understand why he was creating roadblocks in this particular situation and felt unenthusiastic about my opportunity, though. After I dropped out of the competition, Mr. Santini ended up questioning me quite thoroughly about my decision, and I could feel his concern. I could tell that he wanted to be near me, and I wanted to be near him, as well. I didn't share with him the financial limitations in regards to my being on the cheerleading squad, as my pride would never have let me do such a thing. I would never let anyone know that something was not affordable. Instead, I told him about my lack of confidence in making the team, and he told me that he had been assured that I would be a participant. I was disappointed in my decision at that point, I admit, and felt that I had let him down as well as myself.

My parents never discussed my relationship with Mr. Santini with me directly – however, there were a few times that it got their attention. One Valentine's Day, he made an appearance in my history class and presented me with a box of homemade candy. The candy was packaged in a box wrapped in tin foil and it had a hand-cut heart on top, and was filled with homemade dark chocolate filled with cream. It had obviously been given to him by another student, crudely designed as it was. My classmates were delighted with the entertainment of my embarrassment as he presented me with the gift of chocolates. My familiar hot flush of red took over my face as I received the gift, but I treasured the box of candy, as it indicated to me that I was important to him. I could not believe that he was so public in his gesture of affection towards me, and I wondered what the other teacher and students thought about his display of attention.

News about the box of candy incident flew through the small school, and by the time I arrived home, my sister May already knew what had taken place at school that day. She teased me about the candy and shared the information with my mother. I had gone to my bedroom and had taken the box of candy with me so as to not raise any suspicion about my relationship with Mr. Santini, but my mother made a bold entrance into my room and demanded to see the box of candy that Mr. Santini had given to me. I pulled the primitive box out of the closet where I'd hidden it so that she could inspect it as I quickly explained to her that it was an innocent gift which another student had made for him. She asked me some awkward questions about any feelings that I might have been harboring for him, but I denied my romantic feelings and told her that we were just friends. She dropped the questioning and left my room as I wondered what she was really thinking about the situation.

I wasn't bothered by the simplicity of the gift, and I was flattered despite all of the teasing that I endured. I was more irritated with May for letting my mother know about the candy, which exposed that I had some type of relationship with him. Up until that point, there had never been any indication at home that he even existed or was a part of my life.

On another occasion, my parents were asked to give permission for me to attend a large science convention in a nearby city. Mr. Santini had invited me to be his guest along with another teacher and his own student guest. He was excited to explain to me that we could spend the day together, travelling to the city and to the convention; I wanted to go with him on the day trip and tried to envision it.

On my arrival home that day, I shyly asked my parents for permission to attend, and they immediately told me that they would not permit it. I wanted to know the reason behind their decision, and they asked why he didn't call and ask for their permission himself. I didn't know the reason for that and, as a result, I had to tell Mr. Santini that I wasn't allowed to attend. He wasn't happy about the decision and I was embarrassed that I had to decline the invitation. He asked me why my parents felt the way that they did in regards to not letting me attend the convention, and I really didn't have an answer for him, but I think he knew the reason why. When the convention came, I was saddened by the fact that he was away for the day, as he had taken another male student in my place and had let me know who it was that would be spending the day with him.

I knew that Mr. Santini had strong feelings for me, but I really didn't how involved we were until October of my ninth grade year. One day after school, I had a strange sensation come over me and I somehow knew that Mr. Santini was in some type of despair. That night, I worried about his safety and wondered what had caused me to have such a feeling.

The next day in the classroom, I knew that things were different, as there was no eye contact or sense of a special connection coming from him, and it was as though he was intentionally avoiding me. Later that same day, he approached me in the lobby of the school as I was waiting for my sports team practice to begin. We had a very intense conversation in regards to an event that had occurred the previous evening, as he shared with me that he had been involved in a car accident on the way home from school and hat his car had been totaled. It was during that accident when his thoughts had not been about his wife or his child, but about me. His face was filled with serious intent as he told me that he could no longer continue to feel or think about me in the way that he was. My own feelings were immediately hurt, and my heart was broken as it felt a sting of pain. I held back my tears, though, as I could not allow myself to cry in front of him. I felt as though he was blaming me for the way that he felt, and I went home that evening and cried myself to sleep as I wondered why he had told me all the things that he had shared, and then all of a sudden been able to say that he no longer felt the same way.

For the next few weeks, I felt his avoidance, as we saw a lot of movies in his classroom. He would let the film projector roll endlessly as he would leave the classroom unattended. If he was in the classroom teaching class, it was just like any other class, as there was no joking around. Everything seemed to become very serious for him and his behavior changed. There was no stopping in the gym after school and no conversations in the hallway. I missed my relationship with him and wondered how someone my age could have had such an effect on a person like him, and how someone could change so drastically overnight.

I was too shy to approach him and tell him how much I missed our conversations and his attention. I somehow felt betrayed and wondered how someone could seemingly care so deeply and then all of sudden just stop caring, but I secretly scolded myself for not telling him how glad I was that he'd not been injured in the accident. My selfish thoughts were only about me and the loss of someone who had seemed to care about me. At that time in my life, it seemed as though he was the only one that had really cared about me and loved me, despite any of the physical faults I felt that I had. My heart was broken, and I had no one to talk to about how much I cared for my teacher; I couldn't express my true feelings to him because of my own fears, and because he was my teacher and an authority figure, and I was afraid of the consequences. I didn't want to be rejected for any pronouncement of my feelings, as I was already feeling rejected.

Our separation didn't last long, though, as only a few weeks later he appeared in the library where I was on duty as a student librarian. He invited me into a back room of the library which was glassed in and in full sight of other students and the staff librarian. There, he told me that he was unable to stay away from me and that his feelings had not changed. I felt a great sense of relief, but could still not confess my true feelings to him; somehow, though, I think he knew how I felt. Our relationship seemed to be one in which we both felt in tune with each other's feelings. I sometimes felt as though he could read my mind, and that I could almost predict what he was going to say. There have been very few people in my life with whom I have had such synchronicity, truth be told. That day, I realized that he really did care about me even though he had boundaries that he had to respect. I thought about his relationship with his wife and wondered how he was able to carry out his husbandly duties if he felt the way he did about me, but my young mind wasn't fully capable of understanding all of the marital dynamics involved.

At the end of my ninth-grade year, it was a sad moment for me, as I knew that this would be the last time that I would have Mr. Santini as my teacher, though I would still be able to see him in the halls of our junior and senior high school. Prior to the end of that year, he asked me if he could come to the country club to play a game of golf with me, and I knew that I would have to procure permission from my father. This put me on edge because I wasn't sure how he would react. I approached my father, though, and while he was surprised at the request and was hesitant to grant permission, he asked me why Mr. Santini was interested in golfing with me. My response was elusive, as I wasn't sure how to answer such a question. I finally told him that we were friends and that he wanted to spend some time with me. I remember my father giving me an inquiring look then, as if he knew more than what I was sharing. He told me that he needed to think about it for a little bit, as he didn't want to answer me at that moment. After thinking about it for several days, and with another inquiry from me, he finally told me that it would be alright for us to play a game of golf together on the grounds. I could tell from his reaction to my second questioning that he wasn't fond of the idea, though, and he seemed disappointed in my request.

Finally, the last day of my ninth-grade year came and, as I awaited Mr. Santini at my home, I was in a high state of excitement and also feeling some angst about how things were going to go if he was to meet my parents. Regardless of how I felt inside, though, I worked hard to remain calm and not to show any overt emotion that could suggest to my parents how I truly felt about him. I really didn't want him to come inside of our home, as I didn't know how my mother – and, in this case, even my father – was going to react to meeting him. When he pulled into our driveway, I was so anxious that I went out to meet him rather than have him come to the front door.

I felt as though I was on my first date and, realistically, it was a first date for me. It was a cool, dreary day and it was drizzling rain, but neither one of us seemed to mind the elements. We had a fun time and he shared with me that he really didn't enjoy playing golf at all, but had just wanted to have some time alone with me. I felt comfortable on the golf course and we both had an enjoyable time.

While we were out on the golf course that day, he made some suggestions as to where he could take me to be alone on the course as we were playing. He seemed to be looking around as though he were scouting out a place to kiss me. The insinuations were definitely there, but I was not savvy enough to make any recommendations about where we could go to be alone. At one point, he wanted me to help him with his golf swing by wrapping my arms around him; I was frozen with fear, and didn't know how to respond to that request! I was also afraid that my father would find us if I were to make any suggestions, and I was a little fearful as to what might happen if I did.

At the end of the game, we returned to my home and I said my goodbye to him in the driveway. I didn't invite him into our home to meet my parents or my sister May. I saw some type of disappointment on his face, but I wasn't sure what he was feeling at that moment. I was simply sad to say goodbye and see him leave, as we had no other plans to see each other that summer, as we'd had the previous year. I didn't invite him inside, though, because I felt that he really didn't want to meet my father, and I also had some feeling of relief about that since I did not want him to meet my mother.

After Mr. Santini departed, I went inside to find that my mother had the formal dining table all set and had prepared a special meal for him. Both of my parents asked me why I hadn't brought him inside to meet them, but I told them that he'd had to go home to eat dinner with his family. They proceeded to tell me that he was only interested in me for the privilege of playing golf on the private club property. I told them that this wasn't true, and an argument took place as to why he would not want to come inside and have dinner with us. I expressed that we were friends, and that he was not using me to play golf, but my father only pointed out that my mother had prepared a special dinner and spent time getting ready for his appearance. I didn't share with them that I'd been embarrassed about the possibilities of what my mother might or might not do. I also hadn't indicated to her previously that he would be staying for dinner.

I couldn't figure out why they were picking on me and why they had those thoughts about Mr. Santini. At the time, I stood up for Mr. Santini and told them that whatever they thought about him was not true but, looking back, I now realize that it was their attempt to break up any sort of relationship that I had with him. I just wanted to be alone with my thoughts that night, so I quickly ate my dinner and retreated to my room to replay the outing that I had just had with him. Regardless of what my parents thought about the reason for his interest in me, I knew that it was not about playing golf on the country club grounds. I knew that we cared about each other, and I was going to continue to care about him regardless of what my parents thought.

The next three years of senior high were challenging for me, as I didn't see Mr. Santini on a daily basis. He would occasionally catch me in the hallway, stop by the gym, or pull me out of a classroom to chat, though, always reminding me that I was his "number one" and that he still wanted to do "you-know-what" with me. At the end of each year, we would spend a day playing golf at the country club. Each time, I had to ask my father for permission, and every year he was hesitant but always relented.

My father never met Mr. Santini in my presence, but at the end of my junior year I finally invited him into my home and he met my mother. She behaved herself that particular day, and she had few words to say – as he was very gracious and made nice comments about her youthful looks. He also saw my sister May then, who he'd never had her as one of his students. She was scheduled for another science teacher for her eighth and ninth year, but May was well aware of the presence of Mr. Santini in my life, as she had met him at our various sports team practices. He got to know May as my sister finally, though, and she would talk with him in the hallway – it was usually about me, as May would share their discussions with me.

I'm not really sure how much May knew about my relationship with Mr. Santini, as I had not discussed it with her. She knew we were friends, as she would see him talking with me at our after school activities. During my junior and senior years, she even teased me about him when he would show up in the gym to watch our practice or arrive at a game. It was the type of teasing that indicated she knew something, as she would also see us in the hallways having private conversations. In the summer of my senior year, Mr. Santini brought his brother-in-law to play golf with me and May joined us on that outing, but May never directly asked me about him until much later in life.

My senior year was dramatic, as we knew that my college years were approaching and our time together was fast approaching its end. One day, on my way to class, I approached Mr. Santini coming in the opposite direction down the hallway. He pulled me into the Chemistry lab where my Chemistry teacher was the sole occupant of the room. He pushed me up against the chalkboard in front of her and told her that he was in love with me, and she immediately got up out of her chair and rushed to the area where we were standing. She pulled him away from me and told him to behave himself in a demanding voice. He professed his love to me in front of her again, and she told me to leave the room. I was taken aback by his lack of control and that declaration in front of my Chemistry teacher, but I don't know what happened after I left. He'd told her that he was in love with me, and I'd really thought that he was going to attack me, given that he'd had me positioned in a way that would have allowed him to do so.

That same Chemistry teacher had seen us many times talking in the hallway, and I had presented her with my late passes on many other occasions. I'd never had a discussion with her in regards to my relationship with Mr. Santini, but I am sure she was now aware of what may have been taking place. She was the quiet type, though, and I was surprised about how quickly she'd reacted and come to what she thought was my rescue.

After that event, I noticed a change in Mr. Santini's behavior towards me. One day, he stopped me in the hallway and shared with me that he'd been told that he was too friendly with the students. Over the years, I had seen Mr. Santini speaking with other female students in the hallways or after football practice, and I'd wondered if his conversations with them had been similar to the ones he was having with me. If he saw me witnessing any of his conversations with other students, they seemed to stop abruptly and go their separate ways. So, at this time, I thought maybe he had gotten in trouble for talking with someone else. Nevertheless, he indicated to me that he could not spend as much time talking with me as he had, because he didn't want me to think – someday when I was older – that he was an old letch.

The end of my senior year was closing in, and this conversation sent me into a period of depression that revolved around my feelings for him and my upcoming departure from my high school years. I took to my bed for a week and didn't want to go to school or be involved in any of my activities. I really didn't know what to do with myself, truth be told, and I didn't have anyone to talk to about my situation. My mother took me to see our family doctor, and questioned me about the prom and why I wasn't attending; I had been asked by several of my classmates, but just had no desire to go with anyone my own age. My mother and the doctor had a private conversation in which I was not involved, and the subject was dropped. May came home from school with news that Mr. Santini had been asking her about me, and she shared with me that he'd said that I needed to get back to school.

I really had no desire to return to school either, but I made my way back only to have yet another conversation with him that was quite confusing. Upon my return to school, he called me up to the faculty room, where we met outside of the door and had a discussion regarding my future. He told me that I was going to go to college and marry a dentist – because they made a lot of money and I would be happy. In the same breath, he stated that he could never "do you–know-what" with me because it would be all over for him. He told me that, if he touched me, it would be the end of his marriage, and that he loved his wife and his son. Once again, I could feel my face burn with redness at the thought of him indicating that I wanted to marry him. My mind had no thoughts of marriage, even though it was filled with curiosity for what it might have been like to have a physical relationship with him. He had been teasing me for years about the possibility of a physical connection, and all the places where it might take place. I could feel my face turn red with humiliation and the sting of his words piercing my heart. I had no intentions of marrying him, as I had plans to leave that small town and make something of myself, but I just didn't understand his changing behavior and my own feelings, I was so thoroughly confused. I had no words for him at that point, and I turned and walked away with an empty feeling in my heart. I also had feelings of guilt for having had this type of a relationship with a married man, and they played on my mind and soul on a regular basis. I didn't know how to relieve myself of such thoughts.

The next time that I saw Mr. Santini, he invited himself to my home once again for our end of year golf outing. I was surprised that he still wanted to play golf with me and I was confused by the request. The day that he arrived to play golf, both of my parents were away for the day, so I felt comfortable inviting him into the house.

We lived in a big old white country home that was over 100 years old, and the inside was starting to show its age. It had 6 large bedrooms, a country kitchen, and a large front porch with a swing. It was a comfortable home, and I felt fortunate to live in such a beautiful setting. Upon Mr. Santini's arrival, I could see him studying the surroundings in which we lived. My mother had decorated our home with avocado green carpeting which was all the rave of the seventies. Our furniture was of French Provincial design, with wallpaper patterns that were designed to match the décor. I wondered what he thought about the home in which I lived, as I'd often tried to imagine what his own home looked like – but I also knew that I would never know for sure.

Upon his arrival, we proceeded to the course and had a friendly game of golf. He behaved himself through the entirety of the game, until we arrived at the last tee box. As I was standing and preparing to tee up my ball and drive it to the last green, he shared with me that he and his wife were expecting another child. I uttered a congratulatory remark, but I certainly didn't feel that way in my heart. He followed that declaration by telling me that I was his "number one" and that he still wanted to "do you-know-what" with me.

Thoughts raced through my head that I was not supposed to be having, as I was very puzzled and confused – and I really wasn't mature enough to process the information. I didn't know how to respond to someone who was making a declaration about something that didn't correspond with what he was really doing. I was disappointed with his words, in his wanting to be my "number one".

We finished the game in silence and I couldn't bring myself to look him in the face. We returned to my home and I invited him in for a soft drink, and my parents had not returned from their outing. I could hear the hum of the hairdryer coming from the upstairs bathroom, though, and I knew May was in the house. Mr. Santini made a comment about her whereabouts and wanted to know where my bedroom was located; I told him that it was located in the upstairs right-hand corner of our home, and then there was an uncomfortable silence between us.

We both knew that it was time for him to leave and that it would be the last time that I would see him alone prior to going to college. We looked at each other as though a kiss were going to take place, and there was an intense moment of our knowing that, if we did that, it would be the end. Had we kissed, we would have crossed a forbidden boundary that may have changed our lives. In a previous conversation, he had alluded to the fact that there would be no turning back if something got started. In my eyes, we were at that crucial moment as we stared at each other for what seemed like minutes. With hesitation, he told me that he had to leave. He went out the door then, and turned and looked back to take one last look at me, as if to say something else, but he thought better of it. I watched him walk away and my heart was filled with disappointment about the entire situation. I didn't know if he'd been waiting for me to make the first move to give him a goodbye kiss, as I'd thought to myself about what kind of man doesn't make the first move.

I didn't cry after he left even though I felt like it, which itself made me very sad. It was a few days later at my graduation when I had the outpouring of emotion, standing on the stage with my classmates. My peers were all overjoyed to be graduating and moving on to the next stage of their lives. Why I chose that moment to release all of the pent up emotions of the last few weeks is beyond me, but I could no longer hold back the tears as they streamed down my cheeks. I had scanned the audience in the hope that I would see Mr. Santini one last time, and so my mother had made one of her rare public appearances only to see me in tears.

A few days later, I received a graduation card from Mr. Santini with a twenty dollar bill inside. It was signed by him and included the name of his wife, and this time there was no mention of my being his "number one". I knew that he cared about me more than a teacher should care about their student, though.

Through the years, as I have thought back on the time that I spent with Mr. Santini and on my relationship with him, my thoughts and views have been varied. Maturity has changed my perspective and my feelings about his behavior toward me, and my feelings toward him. I have to remind myself that I was an impressionable young lady at the time, and that I was still very innocent to the ways of the world. In retrospect, I somehow feel robbed of my youthful years, in that I did not have any normal childhood. I was so engrossed with Mr. Santini that I placed myself in a fantasy world and didn't enjoy the normal activities of someone my own age. I felt some type of loyalty to him that I didn't understand, but which he unknowingly or knowingly promoted. I didn't go to the prom or date boys my own age because of my feelings toward him.

My psychological involvement with an adult was too intimate for someone of my age at the time, and the confusion that it caused for me in regards to future relationships has had a lasting effect. My having been part of an emotional affair with a married man at such an early age was an act of great trust, and directly affected me developing future relationships with men. There's been significant guilt in knowing that I participated in a betrayal of Mr. Santini's wife and children for all of those years, and in knowing that you can be cheating on someone emotionally as you are fantasizing about someone else.

It took me a long time for me to stop romancing the idea of being with Mr. Santini, long after high school had ended, as it became a daily habit for a span of some twenty-two years over which I had been in communication with him. The secrecy of our relationship was fascinating to me, and I still wonder what attracted me to that type of bond with someone. At that time in my life, I needed to have someone verbally tell me that they cared about me, I suppose, as those words were rarely spoken in my home. I know that my parents loved me, but they did not tell me every day that they loved me.

When you are at that age, you are longing for a relationship of this type – and I was very vulnerable. Having someone tell you on a regular basis that they love you is an attractive thing when you are feeling alone and in need of that type of attention. Mr. Santini was there to provide that for me, regardless of the fact that I was a young girl. I think that, even so soon as when I was sent to the office, he knew that I was the type that was not going to disclose anything, and he was comfortable with the fact that I would not tell anyone about his lack of discretion. That was a test that I passed for him, even though I wished I hadn't.

I have wondered at times if he really did love me, or if he was just physically attracted to a young girl's body. There were other students who I am sure he charmed in the same way over the years, and who I imagine he found great delight in through his involvement with them. I know in my heart that I was not the only one, and that thought turns my stomach. I was so very naïve to think that I was so special to someone like him, only to find out that it was not true. I question how many other young girls may have been his prey in the same way, and I wonder what effects it had on their lives. In hindsight, I should have expressed my feelings to someone in regards to the situation. Bottling up all of the feelings for so many years wasn't good for my emotional well-being, and it took me a long time to break the emotional bond that I'd formed with him – and to be able to have a normal relationship with other men that were better suited for me.

My blemish remained with me for a long time. I finally broke myself away from being in his physical presence, but even then my mind would not permit me to forget him for a long time. I did learn from the experience that "time does heal all wounds."

Years later, it occurred to me that Mr. Santini also had a blemish that he had received somewhere in his life. Maybe it was something that happened in his childhood, or somehow it was a result of his parents' divorce. I will never know what happened to him that would make him want to become involved with someone my age, but I now know that our relationship had something to do with that blemish.

As a result of his blemish, I lost a large part of my childhood and some of the normal activities that I should have been involved in but was too obsessed to take notice of. I had someone who cared about me at a time when I felt that no else did, but I also paid the price for the emotional damage of being involved with someone with whom I should not have been nearly so deeply involved.

In the Classroom – 1983

This is a part of my story that I wish *wasn't* a part of my story. Unfortunately, we don't have the luxury of turning back time and changing the decisions that we have made. I never imagined that one decision could shape the course of your destiny, though, and perhaps I should have. I had the opportunity to escape my small town and the clutches of a man who for some reason had a sort of hold on me. Instead, I made a poor decision in putting myself back in the proximity of someone who I should have placed in my past a long time ago. The choice that I made to return would set off a series of events in regards to my relationships with men that would mark me and my destiny.

I had never planned on returning to my old high school, as I was open to new adventures, but the opportunity almost seemed fated. It was as though Mr. Santini and I had some unfinished business and I was being called on to finish what we had started. Throughout my college years, I had remained in touch with Mr. Santini through written correspondence and an occasional visit back during college breaks. He always stated that he still wanted to "do you–know–what" with me, though I was surprised that he still followed that same line of communication even through my college years. He had an influence on my career, as well, because I had followed in his footsteps and spent my college education studying to become a teacher. I graduated in January of 1981 with a degree in Health and Physical Education, and upon graduation I was invited to take a temporary position in the school district of my alma mater.

I wasn't sure that going back to teach in my old school district was the right thing to do, but I wanted to start my teaching career. I was surprised that I'd gotten an offer so quickly, as teachers weren't in high demand at the time. But, I was lucky, it seemed. My teaching position was located at the other end of the school district from where I'd attended school, but I had also accepted a coaching position in my old junior and senior high school, and so I would be in my old high school gym on a daily basis. The chances that I would see Mr. Santini on a regular basis were pretty significant. I wasn't exactly sure how I felt about the circumstances, but I definitely had some anxiety about the situation.

During my college years, I'd had a few fleeting flirtations, but nothing that led to a commitment of any type. And regardless of how hard I had tried to rid myself of thoughts of Mr. Santini, he still somehow kept a presence in the back of my mind.

My college years *had* produced a more appealing physical appearance for me, but my personality still had some of its same timid personality traits. I had met some nice people in college and had become more confident in developing friendships, but I wasn't sure how comfortable I was going to be with having my old teachers as colleagues. Still, I had finished my student teaching the previous semester in a small college town in Pennsylvania, and now was the real test, as this would be my first solo teaching experience.

Even though I'd be in a familiar school district, being a brand-new substitute teacher proved to be quite a challenge for me. I was a permanent substitute for a popular teacher and I was barely a few years older than the students who I was teaching. I arrived in the middle of a school term and the timing made it difficult to connect with students and faculty, as everyone had already settled into the school term. Simply, I had big shoes to fill, and I found disciplining the male students to be an unproductive effort. There wasn't a huge age difference between myself and the pupils who I was teaching, and I still looked like a high school student myself. The high school principal was retiring that year also, and he didn't particularly care about any troubles that a new teacher was having in his school.

My classroom walls were covered with spitballs that were sent flying through the air when my back was turned. I found frogs in my desk and pin-ups were placed on my movie screen. Comments about my physical attributes were uttered as I walked through the school hallway.

Lunches in the faculty room were very awkward, and I wasn't even made to feel very welcome by the other teachers – lunchtime conversation revolved around their students, and they had no time for anyone who wasn't a permanent fixture. I tried hard to find acceptance amongst the staff, but only found it among a few of the saintlier students. Thankfully, at the end of the day I had my coaching experience to look forward to. I had a wonderful assistant coach and I enjoyed the company of the girls who I had selected for the team.

I was living at home alone with my mother and father at this time, as May had gotten married to a neighbor boy the previous summer and was now expecting a child. The friends that I had made in high school had left the area to attend college and never returned, or else they were busy with raising their own family. Mr. Santini continued to flirt with me sporadically, but somehow I felt all alone. I had immediately reconnected with Mr. Santini on the first day of my teacher orientation, though, which took place prior to my meeting my new students. He was pleased to see me, of course, and immediately started making suggestions about how he would like to "do you-know-what."

I began to realize that he really enjoyed the thrill of talking dirty with me and being in a position where he was able to intimidate me with his words. I could still feel the familiar flush of my face when he confronted me with such a suggestion. Sporadically throughout that first semester, I would encounter him and he would continue with such remarks. I didn't know how I was going to escape the mess that I had gotten myself into with him, but I wasn't meeting anyone my own age to distract me from his attention either, as it was a small town and I already knew there wasn't anyone there who I wanted to date. This added to my dissatisfaction with the circumstances in which I found myself.

My first semester of teaching didn't nearly meet my expectations, and I found myself highly disenchanted with the profession that I had chosen. At the end of my first semester, I decided that I needed to break free of that small town – and so I headed for the Jersey Shore in an attempt to escape the environment in which I'd been living. It would be just a short reprieve for the summer, though, as I soon enough received a phone call for another opportunity coming up in the next semester.

I was called on to return in the fall of the upcoming year for another permanent substitute teaching position and coaching experience. This time, I was going to be teaching junior high students in another building at the same end of the school district. I was hoping that my experience would be different than the one that I'd had the previous year, and from the very beginning, things were a lot different. My fellow staff members were overtly friendly, welcoming, and helpful. I was able to relate a lot better to the age of the students in my classroom, and they seemed to offer me the respect that I desired. The principal was very supportive also, both active and present. This group of faculty seemed to be a closer knit group of people, and very different from the prior staff members who I had encountered.

The male coaches in this building also seemed to be interested in mentoring me, and anxious to include me in their circle. I spent a lot of time in the gym working with them as partners in my new teaching and coaching roles. They also came to my rescue in the classroom with any difficult students who became unruly, and I was thankful for their help and attention. My experience was very different than what I had anticipated, just based on what had happened at the senior high, and I was suddenly able to have more control in the classroom since there was a big enough age difference between myself and the students I taught. I'd become more of an authority figure, and therefore I was able to gain their respect.

I had also accepted another coaching assignment, to coach the junior high girls' basketball team in that building, as well as help with other clubs and organizations that needed teacher supervision. I sailed through the fall semester and was invited back for the spring semester, as the permanent teacher had extended her time off.

Occasionally, Mr. Santini would call over to my building office to speak with me on the telephone. It was as though he needed to hear my voice or just break up his day with a secretive phone call to ask when I would be coming to his building. He'd always end the conversation with some type of sexually suggestive comment. To make matters worse, I would have been called out of my classroom to take any phone call, which caused some suspicion from the office staff who seemed interested in my business. I had to make up some reasons for him to be calling me, and it was an uncomfortable situation really, as I had nowhere to have a private conversation and was conscious of the office staff being in the listening vicinity. It was a small school district, too and news could travel quickly; I was well aware of what they could possibly be thinking about his attentions toward me.

I was also becoming frustrated with Mr. Santini's continual teasing in regards to his suggestions about what he would continually like to do with me. I had gone out with a few local boys who had asked me out on dates, but there was just no interest on my end; they didn't seem to have the ambition or any interests that matched mine. In my mind, I had been formulating my future plans that involved leaving my small town and eventually becoming a business woman, and Mr. Santini was simply a distraction.

But a little romance started to develop between myself and the boy's physical education teacher. We had been teaching classes together and he was the ultimate flirt, always joking around with the girls. He was dark haired and dark eyed with a little boy grin, and he had the build of a wrestler and coached the boy's wrestling team. The rumor was that he was dating another teacher in the senior high and that they had a long term romance going on, but there was no commitment. The first time I'd met him, he'd made some flirtatious remarks and I hadn't quite known how to retaliate, as I'd been taken by surprise.

I found him to be attractive, though, and found myself eating lunch with him in a small room that was off to the side of the cafeteria on a daily basis. His name was Dan and he was quite a few years older than myself. Our conversations were friendly and I soon developed a little crush on him. I even started bringing some home-made baked goods to share with him at lunch time. During the winter months, he invited me to help him chaperone the ski club with which he was involved, and he taught me the basics of skiing since I had never skied before, even though I'd lived in the mountains of Pennsylvania and had had access to several ski resorts.

He was patient with me with the lessons, as I could be quite clumsy with my feet despite my athleticism. We had a lot of fun on the ski slopes and I was grateful for the lessons that he gave me; I enjoyed the challenge of skiing, and ended up spending time on the slopes even many years later. My thoughts on us were that he enjoyed teaching me, and I was encouraged that he might ask me out on a date.

In the spring of that year, I gained enough confidence to invite him to play a game of golf with me on the club property. He accepted the invite, to my surprise, and arrived one afternoon when the weather seemed to be questionable. Sure enough, in the middle of the game, a thunderstorm started and we continued to play – against my better judgement. My father had always taught me to evacuate the course at any sign of lightning, and I indicated to Dan that we should take cover, but he wanted to continue with the game. Not long after this, my father arrived in a golf cart to retrieve us, and he was not pleased. He told us to leave the course immediately, and Dan took off for his home – clearly feeling a bit sheepish.

In the conversation I had with my father afterwards, he shared with me that he didn't think that Dan was very bright and that he was disappointed with my judgement about not getting off of the golf course when an electrical storm was taking place. I tried to defend Dan to my father, but I knew from previous experience that he wasn't likely to change his mind about Dan's lack of common sense.

It was coming close to the end of the school year when Dan invited me to play tennis with him and another couple one Saturday afternoon. I was surprised by the invite because the rumor was that this was the spot his petite blonde girlfriend filled on a regular basis. He did share with me that she wasn't available that particular

Saturday, but I still wasn't sure of the status of their relationship and didn't really feel inclined to pry into his personal business. Thus, I graciously accepted the invitation, as I was somewhat skilled in the game of tennis and thought it was an opportunity to become closer to Dan. I wasn't sure of his romantic circumstances anyway, I reminded myself, and just accepted it as an opportunity to get to know him better – in spite of what my father thought about him.

The day of the date, I was dressed inappropriately, as everyone else had on their tennis whites and I arrived in a basic pair of shorts and a tank top. I'd brought along a change of clothes as we were going to dinner afterwards, though, and we went to a very nice restaurant; I felt out of place, unfortunately, as the other couple seemed quite worldly and of a higher social bracket. They were delightful actually, but I felt that maybe Dan was a bit embarrassed by me and my lack of social grace at the time.

After dinner, we arrived back at his apartment and he told me that I needed to stay over, as I'd had two glasses of alcohol and it was a forty-five-minute drive for me to get home. I told him that I needed to call and let my parents know that I wouldn't be coming home that evening, as they were expecting me, but I was nervous about calling my home to tell my parents that I was going to spend the night at his apartment. My mother answered the phone, and without much explanation she responded that it was okay. It was very short and to the point, and we hung up the phone. No questions asked.

Dan only had the one bed, so I assumed that I was going to sleep with him – and, surprisingly, I wasn't nervous. I hadn't really given it any thought, truth be told, and I was tipsy from the small amount of alcohol I'd had earlier in the evening. Soft music was playing from his bedside radio as I crawled into the bed beside him. I was in my underwear, which he slowly removed as he caressed me and kissed me softly on the lips. Our sexual exploration was all over with before I even knew what had really happened. He used protection, and I didn't find it to be either pleasant or unpleasant. Prior to falling asleep, he told me that I was beautiful and that any man would be happy to be with me. I felt content, and slept well snuggled in his arms in his small apartment bed that evening. I felt as though he had some feelings for me and thought that he did care for me.

The next morning, I got up and got dressed, and I left his apartment without breakfast or a kiss goodbye. Instead, I thanked him for the nice time and told him that I would see him at school on Monday. On the drive home, I thought about Mr. Santini and how he could now no longer be my number one.

I don't know why I decided to sleep with Dan. I know that I was extremely lonely; and I was attracted to him, but I was not in love with him. Thinking back, I've thought that perhaps he thought I had slept with other men as a result of a college experience. I was almost twenty-four at the time. I'd been wanting to have a sexual relationship, as I was starting to feel like an oddball in that respect, but I had wanted it to be with the right person.

I didn't share my experience with Dan with anyone – mainly because I had no one to really share with, as my high school friends were no longer around and I didn't have anyone who was close by to confide in. The following Monday when I saw Dan at school, he was friendly and I was a bit embarrassed, as I didn't know what he must have thought about me sleeping with him so easily. He acted as though nothing had happened, and yet I had expectations of being asked out on another date. I really didn't know what to think, though, and all I could think of was my mother once saying, one time, "Why buy the cow when you can get the milk for free?" I hadn't been sure what she meant at the time, but now I thought that I did. I changed my mind about him possibly caring for me, though, as his actions didn't indicate to me that he really did. I found it to be hurtful, and difficult to understand. Was he blemished because he was ashamed of what he had done? And what was his situation with his girlfriend?

My mother had not said a word to me about spending the night with Dan, and neither did my father. They may have wondered about the situation, but I guess they were having enough of their own problems to be concerned about mine.

Shortly after this happened, I was chaperoning a dance one Friday night when I was approached by Mickey, the attending school principal. He was a regular chaperone for the Friday evening school dances and, with his being my immediate supervisor, I had gotten to know him a little bit. He was a bit intimidating to the students and staff because he could be somewhat overbearing, given him being quite a disciplinarian who took care of any problems with a stern hand. He was married, and had a son who was a student in the same school. His wife was a teacher in the school district, as well, and taught in my old high school. She had arrived after I'd left, though, so I'd never had her for class even though I was now aware of who she was.

Dan had shared with me that he'd had some differences with Mickey as a result of their shared coaching responsibilities. I wasn't privy to what the differences were, but I was aware of the friction. Thinking back on the entire situation from my current perspective, I realize I was surrounded by a lot of male testosterone, as well as male ego, and some bumping of heads had been taking place.

This particular Friday evening, Mickey invited me out for a drink after the dance at a local tavern. I accepted the offer, as I had nothing else going on and was still miffed about Dan not following up with me for another date invite. The evening with Mickey was a friendly and enjoyable visit, as he dropped me back at my car with nothing of a sexual nature having transpired. A few weeks later, I chaperoned another dance and Mickey asked me once again to join him for a drink. Once again, it was all quite innocent and I was returned to my car without any uncomfortable incidences.

A week later, I was scheduled by Mickey to attend a school conference at a convention center in a nearby city. Mickey would also be attending the conference along with a few other teachers from the school district. We drove separately and spent the day listening to various topics regarding education, and a dinner followed. That evening, I joined him and the other teachers in the bar for a drink afterwards. I had a feeling that Mickey was becoming attracted to me as the evening progressed, as he started giving me a lot of attention and was purchasing my drinks. I found myself drinking a little more than I should have, though, and I wasn't very good at holding my liquor. I retired to my room early, and any intentions that Mickey may have held regarding the overnight stay at the convention center were, in my mind, also put to rest.

The school year was coming to a close and I had no plans for the summer except to serve ice cream in a local dairy mart. I'd been asked to come back in the fall as a day-to-day substitute teacher so that I could continue my coaching assignments, as the regular teacher would be returning to her old position. Thus, at least for the moment, I planned to stay in the area.

My personal plans for the summer involved actively pursuing a teaching position elsewhere, as well as working at that local dairy mart to make some extra cash. In spite of my plans to look elsewhere, though, I'd accepted my coaching roles and the plan for my being a substitute teacher for the entirety of the school district on a day-to-day basis, as called upon to be available. This meant that, on any given day, I would receive a call at five o'clock in the morning to go step into any role for any teacher who had called off sick.

Over that summer, I searched frantically to find another job that would allow me to be a full-time teacher. I went on several interviews, but wasn't successful in being offered a permanent teaching position. I even travelled quite a distance for a few of the interviews, but without any offers being extended. I had some worries about the fall semester and how much work I would actually be offered as a substitute teacher. I would be making forty dollars a day, plus a small lump sum payment in return for my coaching duties, but this was minimal. The fall semester arrived without any new offer, though, and to my surprise, I was called on a fairly regular basis to teach. If teaching is what you would like to call my services that year. It was more like babysitting a classroom of students. Most of the time, there was no lesson plan and I was left on my own to become quite creative in the way of entertaining them for the class period. Nevertheless, it was employment, and I was able to keep my foot in the door for any permanent opportunities that might arise.

I was frequently called to the junior high where I just had my last teaching experience, and also to my old alma mater where Mr.

Santini was based. Mickey indicated to me that he'd requested that I be called first to his school, and so I thanked him for keeping me busy and helping me to stay employed. I saw Mr. Santini more frequently, and talked with him on a regular basis. He even requested me as a substitute when he went missing from his classroom. It felt strange to sit in his classroom and sit at that desk that he used on a daily basis; I was tempted to snoop through his desk, but resisted the urge.

I also saw Dan and Mickey at the junior high while teaching there and while taking care of my coaching responsibilities. Dan would flirt with me on occasion, but nothing more than that would transpire. Once again, I enjoyed my coaching experience and loved working with the girls who I coached. The girls on the team put in the work and as a result we had a successful season. At the end of the semester, I was invited to the junior high staff Christmas party at a local tavern, and Mickey encouraged me to attend along with a few of the other female staff members. I had reservations about going, as I wasn't really a member of their staff, but they made me feel welcome. My gut was trying to tell me something, though, and I should have heeded its advice. I arrived around 4 o'clock, after school, where a seat had been saved for me by Dan, Mickey, and a few of the other male staff members. The guys immediately started buying me drinks and, before I knew it, I was a bit intoxicated.

My experience with alcohol was really quite limited, and when it came time for me to leave the party I could hardly stand up from the bar. It was time for me to go home, and I wasn't fit to drive my car home. There was some discussion amongst the men as to who was going to drive me home, and I protested that I would call my father and he would come and get me to take me home without problems, but Mickey kept insisting that he didn't live far from my home and that he'd be the one to drive me. The rest of the men seemed to be comfortable with that decision, as he was the principal, after all. I was disappointed in Dan, as he made no attempt to rescue me from the situation or offer to take me home.

Mickey drove a truck, and he assisted me up into the cab, as I was weak in the knees. We had no sooner driven out of the parking lot than

Mickey asked me if I had ever been to a strip club. I wasn't interested in going to a strip club, but felt a bit intimidated by the situation. He told me that I needed to have the experience and off we went. He drove about forty-five minutes to a club near a shopping mall that I frequented. Once we arrived at the club, I knew immediately that I didn't want to be there. I recall that I had another drink despite my better judgement, and I was quite worried about seeing someone who I knew. I can't imagine who that might have been, but I remember it being a concern.

I don't know how long we stayed at that club and I don't remember too much of what I saw, except in that I felt very uncomfortable. When we got back into Mickey's truck, I know that I felt very sick, as I had the bitter taste of vomit in my mouth. The next thing that I knew, I had thrown up all over a new light blue winter nylon jacket that I was wearing and was trying to open the truck door. Mickey tried to help me clean up and actually found it to be quite humorous. I didn't feel well, though, and I wanted to go home, and I didn't want to be in this situation.

Through my queasiness and ill feelings, I gave him directions to my home. It didn't take much, as he seemed to already know where I lived. He dropped me off in front of my home at well past midnight. I was nervous about what my parents would think about my vomit-stained jacket and my late arrival, but thankfully, no one was waiting up for me and there seemed to be no concern about my whereabouts.

It was a Friday evening and May's car was in the driveway, as she had arrived home for the holidays. I took off my jacket and placed it in the washing machine so as to wash away the evidence of my misconduct, and then I went up to my bedroom and laid down on my bed, which seemed to spin for hours. I was worried how I was going to recover my car that had been left in the tavern parking lot.

The next morning, I caught May in the living room before entering the kitchen where my mother was seated. I told her that we needed to go and retrieve my car, and that she needed to help me get out of the house and go get it. I told her that I had gotten drunk and that I had thrown up all over my jacket that was now in the washing machine. May started to laugh and knew that I had gotten myself into some sort of trouble; I could feel her sense of pleasure in the situation, as I had never gotten in any sort of trouble during my high school years. She had often referred to me as a goody-two-shoes. She couldn't wait to hear the details regarding my previous evening, and so we made an excuse about needing to pick something up at the store and headed out the door.

On our way to retrieve my car, I didn't tell her about the strip club or who I had actually been with the previous evening. I didn't even share with her about sleeping with Dan or about the attention of Mickey. I just said that I'd gotten drunk at the party and gotten sick on my jacket. I told her that a fellow female colleague had brought me home, as I didn't want her to think poorly of me, her older sister.

After the holidays and my next teaching assignment in Mickey's school, he hunted me down and asked me how I was doing. I was surprised by his care and concern, as it was so different from what I had experienced with Dan. He seemed to truly be concerned about me and wanted to know if I would chaperone the next dance at the school. I thought about declining because I didn't want to encourage anything, but found myself giving him an affirmative answer anyway. I already sensed that he was going to ask me to go for a drink afterwards, and somehow I just wasn't able to refuse.

And then, I was starting to enjoy his attention. At the bar, he would ask me the questions that no one else seemed to really care about. He would ask me about my life and my childhood, and the things that no one else really understood about me. The alcohol would somehow consume me and make me oblivious to my surroundings, and best of all it would make me feel numb to the loneliness that I was feeling. I didn't share the details regarding my mother, but told him a few select things about my family.

We usually went to some off the hidden path bar where he would choose to take me, and we would talk and play video games for most of the evening. I asked about his marriage and he shared that his wife didn't care anymore, and that their relationship was strained. I had feelings of guilt for taking him away from his family, and I wondered about his wife and what she must have thought about him coming home smelling like beer, and if she gave any thought to his whereabouts. I questioned what had blemished their marriage to make Mickey seek out companionship from me.

At the end of that evening, he gave me a kiss and I knew that it was the beginning of something more meaningful. Over the next few weeks, we made plans to see other on a regular basis, as he would make plans to meet me at a predetermined location. I would leave my car in some out of the way parking area and he would come and pick me up. I would make up some story for my parents to justify my time out of the house, but they didn't ever question me about how my time was being spent.

It became almost routine, once or twice a week, for us to get drunk, play video games, and have a petting session in his truck afterward. I remember the numb feeling that I had that seemed to go away with each sip of alcohol that I was drinking at his expense. There were many times when I maneuvered my car down the winding narrow icy mountain roads that winter and early spring, and in the late hours of the evening, having indulged far too much. I am only grateful that I didn't have an accident and injure myself or anyone else.

It was evident that Mickey was becoming more interested in me, as I was with him. He wanted to meet more often, and skipped school in the afternoons when I wasn't teaching or coaching in order to see me. One day, he took me to see where he'd grown up and I knew that things were becoming more serious than I'd so far imagined. I didn't feel good about what we were doing, even though we had not had full sexual relations, but we were discussing a night in a hotel room. I felt guilt when I thought about us, and was incessantly worried about being discovered. I was starting to feel paranoid also, and I knew that I wanted to confide with someone, but didn't know in whom I could confide.

Our discussions had turned toward spending an evening in a motel room, as I mentioned, and one evening after some discussion, we agreed on a place and a time. We met one evening at a bar and got drunk. I was nervous about the situation and feeling hesitant.

We went to the motel, where Mickey checked in while I waited in the truck. We were both very nervous and the evening didn't go as planned – an attempt was made, but we were both overcome with alcohol. I wondered about his wife and son, and couldn't help but think about Mr. Santini, as he had talked with me often about this same plan. I wondered if he might be disappointed if he knew about my current affair.

I thought about my parents, and how disappointed they would be that I had put myself in such a situation. I thought about the church that I attended and how God might view my actions. I knew that I was going to go straight to hell for having this encounter with a married man. And after this encounter, my feelings of guilt became overwhelming, and Mickey's interest in me became more intense.

He started to discuss with me the possibility of leaving his wife so that the two of us could leave town and get married. Yet, I wasn't interested in getting married to him or to anyone for that matter, and I didn't want someone to leave their wife for me. I wasn't ready to make a commitment, and this all sounded very serious to me. From what I had seen in regards to marriage, truth be told, it was something that I really didn't want any part of at that moment in my life.

One afternoon, Mickey left a letter on my car windshield, asking me to meet him to discuss a commitment. When I read the letter, I was overcome with intense fear regarding what I had done. I didn't want to marry him and I didn't want to ruin his marriage. I didn't show up at the meeting place that he'd suggested. He called my home to inquire about my whereabouts, though, and I even felt as though he had driven past my home. I couldn't and didn't give him any explanation about my behavior, but I am sure that he couldn't understand my change of mind.

Things had gotten very involved, and I was aware that other people might suspect that we were having an affair. I'd let my feelings get the best of me, and I was finally about to burst with the intensity of my feelings. I was also concerned that Mr. Santini would hear about my indiscretions, and I wasn't sure what he would think.

While on a teaching assignment, I was placed in the same study hall as Mr. Santini, and our close proximity permitted us time to sit down and talk with each other. Whether it was because of the similarity of the situation that I was in with Mickey, or just a build-up of all of the promises from Mr. Santini, I suddenly felt compelled to share the details of my affair with him.

Over all of the years that we had known each other, I'd never felt so inclined to say something to him as I did at that moment. I don't know whether it was based in my own personal paranoia about the situation or just the deep need to share with someone that I trusted, but I guess I just wanted someone to tell me that everything was going to be alright. It all came tumbling out of my mouth so easily that I felt a great sense of relief, as if I was releasing myself from carrying a burden that I had been carrying for many years. I will not say that the look on his face was rewarding to me, however, as it was not. I could see the hurt come across his face, along with a sense of disbelief that I would do such a thing.

I could see the tears build up in his eyes and I knew that I had hurt him more than I'd ever intended. I'm not sure that my blurting out my personal affairs was intentional, and rather think it was more about my needing someone to care about me. Someone to care enough to say that I really needed to stop this type of behavior. I was looking for someone to care about me as much as I cared about them, and out of all the people in the world, I'd thought that person would have been him.

The reaction to my revelation was not what I imagined, though, and while I hadn't planned to tell him, he had pushed my buttons. He asked me then, "How could you have done that? You didn't sleep with me, but you slept with someone else?" For my part, I couldn't believe what I was hearing, and I didn't have any response for him. The bell rang and ended our intense conversation then, and we went our separate ways.

Two weeks later, Mr. Santini ended up in the hospital with a bleeding ulcer, and he wouldn't return to school for two months. I really don't know that the bleeding ulcer had anything to do with the

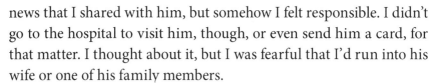

news that I shared with him, but somehow I felt responsible. I didn't go to the hospital to visit him, though, or even send him a card, for that matter. I thought about it, but I was fearful that I'd run into his wife or one of his family members.

After he returned to school, he asked me why I hadn't visited him or sent him a card. All that I could say was that I was sorry.

I would only see Mr. Santini in person two more times. The first time, I was substitute teaching for the woodshop teacher. I was sitting at the desk in front of the classroom when Mr. Santini expectantly arrived in my classroom. Unbelievably, he reached down and put his hands between my legs as I sat on my chair behind the desk. The jean skirt that I was wearing had a slit up the front and was accompanied by a pair of tall boots. He made it to appear as though he was getting into my desk drawer, but he was fondling my private area instead.

The young lady sitting directly in front of me looked at my face as though she knew what was going on. Upon his request, I excused myself from the classroom to follow him out to the vacant adjoining shop area, and there he pushed me into a corner. He started to talk dirty to me and I became fearful that we would be caught in such a compromising position, but just as I thought something was about to happen, the bell rang for the class to end and he released me from his grip. He quickly backed off as the students started to file out of the classroom, and left me standing dumbfounded as he disappeared out into the hallway. I was shocked by the encounter, and left puzzled by what had just happened.

The next time that I saw Mr. Santini was the last time that I would ever see him. It was a few weeks later and the last week of the school year. I was sitting all alone in the women's faculty room during a free period when once again I was surprised by his entrance. I didn't know how he'd known where I was or that I was alone. He came into the lounge and sat directly across from me, and started to interview me as though he was a psychologist interrogating a patient. I stared back at him and answered the questions with a face that masked the emotions that I was really feeling.

He asked me about my relationship with Mickey, and I told him that it had ended, sharing how it had happened. I also told him about my short relationship with Dan, and I relayed to him that I was never getting married and that I was never having children. He questioned me about that decision, and I think that he felt the hardness of my heart that had developed as a result of the relationships which had left their blemishes. He had tortured my mind for years, though, and I wondered if he now wanted to be absolved of his deeds.

He got up from his chair and came over to me as if to kiss me, because our faces were that close. But instead, he placed his hands down into the loose-fitting corduroy slacks that I was wearing. I wanted to kiss him, truth be told, but I was afraid of what would happen. His hands went down into my underpants for just a few moments as the change of class bell rang once again, and with that he quickly removed his hands from me and went into the washroom situated behind me. It was just in the nick of time, too, as a fellow female staff member had just entered the room as he went. That was the last time that I ever saw Mr. Santini.

Upon my exit from the teacher lounge that day, I decided that it really was time for me to move on. I knew that, if I continued to work in that school district, I was going to be held captive in the game that Mr. Santini and I were playing with each other. It was as though an immediate knowing came over me, that if I did not physically separate myself from him, I was going to be caught in this emotional affair for the rest of my life. I made up my mind that, no matter what, I was not going back to teach in that school district the following year. Somehow, I was going to leave that small town and start my life over. It was not clear how I was going to do it, but I made up my mind that I needed to move on, and that I was going to do it. I was glad that it was the last week of the school year, as I felt a great weight lift off of my shoulders as I made my way out of the building.

It truly was the last time that I saw Mr. Santini, though it was not the last time that I ever heard from him. Several years later, he called me at my apartment on a snowy winter day. I'd been unable to get to my job that particular morning due to the icy and snowy conditions. I was working in the city at the time, and lived quite a distance from my workplace. Mr. Santini somehow procured my phone number and called me at home early that morning. On the phone, he shared with me that he'd been hoping that I would be at home. I was taken by surprise, as I hadn't been expecting to hear from him ever again. He seemed to be in some state of mind where he was quite adamant about the need to see me. Several times, he asked me to come to the school to visit with him, saying he needed to talk with me. He would not tell me over the phone what seemed to be the problem in regards to the urgency.

In my apartment, I wasn't moved by his request, as I was in a relationship with someone and didn't wish to destroy it. I listened to his request and didn't indicate to him one way or another as to whether I would make that visit. However, in my heart, I knew that I had no intentions of ever seeing him again, as I didn't want to reignite my involvement with him. For some reason, I remained on the phone to listen to him, but I ended the conversation with no commitment. What compelled him to call me that particular day, I will never really know, but I do know that it had something more to do with him than it had to do with me.

In January of 1995, twenty-two years after I met Mr. Santini, I would hear from him for the last time. Two days after my marriage to my now husband, I received a call at my workplace in Pittsburgh. My secretary answered the phone and transferred it to my desk. In the small town where I grew up, news travels fast, and he'd heard that I'd gotten married that previous weekend. I was under the presumption that he was calling to ask me about the marriage, but instead, he made a smart comment about my having my own secretary and how I must be somebody important. During our last meeting, I had told him that I was never getting married. His words to me on this call were, "I thought you were never getting married," as though he'd really expected me to remain single for the rest of my life. In that moment, I told him that I was happy and that I had met someone who I wanted to marry. To my dismay, what had seemed like a simple conversation turned to one where he started to talk dirty to me in a desperate attempt to renew our old relationship – telling me about the porn he liked to watch in a hotel room, as I had told him that I traveled quite frequently with my job. I made no response to his inappropriate remarks and remained silent. He then told me that he would be in the hotel that was located in my building for a convention in Pittsburgh the following month. He made a suggestion that we could meet for a drink, but I once again made no indication that I was interested in seeing him, and I felt disgusting for even having a conversation with him. I told him with a direct tone that I was happy then, and the conversation came to an end. That was the last time that I ever heard from Mr. Santini.

After that telephone conversation, I felt a sense of relief at finally being free of something that I had been carrying around for a long time. My relationship with him had finally come to a conclusion. At that moment, I *was* finally free, and I was free to be happy in the relationship with my new husband. The decision that I had made many years earlier to return to my alma mater had changed the course of my life, but I'd overcome that decision. In retrospect, I see now that the more important decision I made was to step away from the situation, and to start all over in order to survive. The bond that had held me there was finally broken, but I was not.

With sad disappointment, I now think back about my experiences in the classrooms of my old alma mater and the relationships that I developed there. The choices that I made left me with a permanent stain as a result of my loneliness and my need to be loved by someone. Thinking back on that time in my life, I see that learning to place boundaries on who you allow into your life and why seems to be a prominent theme. It took me a long time to learn how to distinguish good from bad in that respect. It shouldn't be easy for just anyone to cross the threshold into my heart, but with my being young and inexperienced then, I hadn't yet learned that loving just anyone leaves heavy marks and scars that come with the high price tag of being broken hearted.

Regardless of the decision that I made to return to my small town, and the snowball of poor choices to follow in regards to my relationships with men, I learned that you cannot go back in time and change your decisions – but you can work to make better decisions in the future. My time in the classroom was just the beginning of the lessons that I would learn in regards to love and relationships of all types.

Martin & Terri

Based on the experiences that I'd had in my old school district, I'd been left wondering what my future would hold in regards to my romantic life, as well as my future in general. I realized that I'd let fate place men and situations in my life rather than pursue anything of real value on my own accord, as my string of negative relationships had so far brewed nothing more than unwanted trouble for myself. In 1985, I finally broke free by leaving the situation in an attempt to start fresh, but it would be ten more years before I'd finally meet a wonderful man and get married after overcoming some very deep challenges. In retrospect, though, the real turning point came in 1985 when I got involved in two very different relationships that would shape my destiny in new ways.

But before I get to those relationships, I need to tell you about my brother Martin and the woman who he brought into my life. Her importance to my story lies in the fact that she'd not only add a long-lasting imprint to my already scarred heart, but would also leave a blemish on not only myself, but on my brother.

The relationship that she had with my brother would end up bringing to light some harsh facts about the reality of love relationships, and only with her presence would they come to the forefront for me. Up to this point, the only real love relationship that I had paid much attention to had been that of my mother and father. My father was so deeply devoted to my mother even though they had rough patches; he was simply very much committed to her. I had not really seen anything out of the ordinary in regards to love relationships up to this point – at least as far as I knew – but that was all about to change.

When Martin met Terri, I was twelve years old, and it was just about the time when my mind was thinking about puppy love. I was in the seventh grade and Martin was living with us at this point, as he had just returned from his duty in the army. He only lived with us for a short time, until he got his electrician job, and then he moved into a place of his own. Supposedly, my brother had some help from my mother in securing such a good job. During her dating years, my mother had dated one of the then plant managers, and so she called him for his assistance. I admit, this information caused some dissention between my other brother William and my mother for years, as she hadn't made the same phone call for him. This was something that my brother William would remember for years later, as he felt my mother favored Martin over him. I'll share more about this disagreement later on, as this impacted by brother William's relationship with me and also with our entire family for a long time to come. But on the subject of Martin... I adored my brother Martin, as we were very close, and I wanted to make sure that he married the perfect woman. I wanted him to get married and to be happy, as I still romanticized marriage at that time, and I remember the first time that I met his wife Terri – as I gave her a good evaluation. During our first meeting, I took notice of her long dark hair, as it was parted in the middle and I wasn't sure it suited her heart-shaped face. After their marriage, she got it cut with layers and had it feathered so that it was more flattering to her, but that straight cut was what first struck me about her. She had a peculiar nose which she even made fun of herself, and she would sometimes press down on it and laugh. Light tan freckles sparkled over her entire body as they appeared against her pale skin. Most importantly, she laughed with ease at some of the same silly things that I enjoyed.

Terri was seven years younger than Martin, as she had just graduated from high school when they started dating. My brother Martin had been in the army and, upon his return, gotten a great job as an electrician at a local power plant. His stars seemed aligned, as all of the important moments in life were happening for him in the correct order. It seemed as though he proposed to Terri almost immediately, as I don't recall their dating that long before the announcement of their engagement.

In the early days of their dating, Terri seemed a bit uncomfortable in the confines of our home, as she would more often than not pick up a magazine from the coffee table to read. She would absorb herself in the magazine as if to lose awareness of everything going on around her. I really didn't blame her, though, as my mother wasn't easy to make conversation with, and my sister and I gawked at her as if she was nothing more than a new and interesting distraction. Early on, I wasn't sure how much she knew about my mother, as her introduction to us came about a year or so prior to my mother's formal diagnosis. With that being said, I am sure that Terri had an inkling that something was just not right. It took her a while to warm up to my sister and I also, as we were a bit reserved when she was in our presence.

I remember being a little bit jealous of her attention from my brother Martin, as I always looked up to him. His appearance was a lot like that of my father – tall with dark hair – but he had a slightly heavier body build as compared to the slimness of my father. He was very nice looking, and had a nice personality to match. Martin would go out of his way to help anyone, and he seemed to have a number of friends that he hung out with at the time. He was generous with my sister and I also, as he would treat us to ice cream or buy us a new record – in fact, we especially shared the love of music. Martin and I would spend Saturday afternoons listening to Casey Kasem's top forty countdown on the radio. He had purchased a large tape recorder, and we would religiously tape all of the top hits together.

Martin was easy to favor, as he was very easy-going and likeable, and we got along well together. In my eyes, Martin and Terri seemed like the perfect couple, and I grew to like Terri very much. They settled in easily together and were soon living a nice country lifestyle, having purchased a piece of land not far from my parents' home, as they were starting to build their own home that was complete with a garden. My brother was very talented, and was able to do a lot of the work himself. When they started the actual building process, I helped to do a little bit of the manual labor as my brother provided me with instructions. Terri enjoyed that type of work, as well, and we would work side by side on the development of their home.

It was during my junior and senior years in high school when Terri and I became even closer, as she helped me to secure my first job at that local dairy mart I mentioned earlier. Terri worked there with her sister, and later on May also joined us. The four of us had a lot of fun laughing together in the small space in which we maneuvered to make fast food and ice cream delights for the patrons. The couple who owned the place were rather intense in their management, and we would find them to be quite entertaining. I made some errors in preparing some of the orders and had to find some creative ways to dispose of them without the owners getting upset! I would go home with my work smock stuffed with rolled-up napkins full of burnt hamburger pieces and French fries, as I learned early on to take my cooking mistakes home with me – the owner would go ballistic if he found them in the trash can. I had to be a little creative in how to get rid of them, as we would often hear Mr. Sawyer bellowing in the back room about any waste that would take place. Mrs. Sawyer would bounce around like a bumble bee in the small quarters, and almost knock us over in order to get her orders out in a timely manner.

I spent my summers during college working with Terri, and the more time that we spent together, the more she became like an older sister to me – and at times, she was like a mother. We would spend our days off going to the movies, swimming in the club pool, making new recipes, and engaging in other fun activities. She opened up a whole new world to me as she helped me to shop for clothes to wear, gave me advice in regards to makeup, and even helped me pick out my glasses. She helped me with the things that a mother would typically help her daughter with.

Terri would also make fun of my mother and the soap operas that she was obsessed with watching. We had watched "the shows" every summer, right on from when we were in grade school and on through high school. It was Terri who told me how silly it was to spend so much time being engaged in the love affairs of the various characters. She encouraged May and I to spend more time swimming at the pool and enjoying our presence in the outdoors rather than being entrapped in the fantasy world of the soap operas. My mother watched the same soap opera every day for most of her married life, though, and it was almost common practice to watch it with her.

Terri was all about enjoying the present moment and celebrating the special occasions in life, and it was Terri who planned my high school graduation party and presented me with roses and a cake on my big day. I hadn't been expecting anything at the end of my ceremony, and on my arrival home I was surprised with a party. I loved her for her kindness and generosity in thinking about me, and I couldn't believe that someone cared enough to do something so nice.

I spent a lot of time with her in those years prior to college and then during my summers home from school. She helped me to prepare for college by helping me to shop for what I needed even though she had never attended college herself. And once I left for college, she decided to go back to school to become a medical secretary. She went to a local college for two years and, upon graduation, got a job at the local hospital. Martin and Terri only came to my college one time, they stayed so busy, and that was after I had an injury that required surgery. It was Terri who came to my rescue in a time when I needed someone the most.

It was in February of my sophomore year when I had an accident playing intramural basketball. I had a very heavy ball come down on my left middle finger, jamming it backwards. At the time, I thought that I had just stubbed it, but a few days later I realized that something more serious had occurred. After a trip to the college infirmary, I was informed that I had fractured it and that I needed to have surgery for the repair. I was in quite a situation at that point, as the infirmary physician arranged for me to go to a hospital in the city to have the surgery. The hospital was about an hour and a half's drive away, and I had no transportation at the time. My timing wasn't great either, as my parents were in Florida on their annual vacation. After discussing this with my college friends, I was relieved that a few of them could plan accordingly and arrange to get me to the hospital.

It was a snowy, dreary day in the midst of winter, but they took time away from their classes to navigate our way to a strange part of the city. It was my best friend and two of our guy friends who drove me there and dropped me off in front of the hospital. I was nervous about the entire situation, as it was all a new experience for me, and I wasn't particularly fond of the idea of having an operation and having to spend several days in a hospital afterwards. I remember that the nurses and doctors were extremely nice to me, and questioned me about the whereabouts of my parents, family, and friends since I'd been left all alone. The night prior to the surgery, I silently cried myself to sleep, frightened and feeling a bit sorry for myself in my loneliness. My parents had of course called me from Florida to apologize for not being there, and my best friend's mother had sent me flowers, but I was scared. My fractured finger needed to have a pin placed through the first knuckle. I spent several days in the hospital and received great treatment from the staff, as I was in some pain.

It was Terri who came to bring me home from the hospital. She took me home for the weekend to recuperate before driving me the four hours back to school. I remember being so happy to see her, and grateful for her help.

Upon my return to campus, I had to walk around with my left middle finger all bandaged up with a splint and had to keep my finger raised in the air with the help of a sling. On the funnier side of this, I never gave so many people the middle finger in all of my life! It was all very embarrassing, and I think everyone on my college campus knew who I was as a result. I was very happy when the day came that my father arrived on campus to take me back to see my doctor and have the dressing removed. My left middle finger, as a result of that injury, has a slight bend at that joint, as it never fully straightened out. It was permanently blemished as a result of the injury, but it was not broken.

Terri was instrumental in not only caring for me, but also in caring for the rest of our family. During the times when my mother was institutionalized, she would help to make sure that we had food to eat. She would bring something to the house or have us over to their home for dinner. She seemed to understand that my mother was different and that she could help to provide my sister and I with some guidance. Terri also brought some fun into my life, as she took me to my first concert. She knew that I loved The Carpenters, and it was she and Martin who surprised me with tickets to that first concert. I have never forgotten the joy I experienced, listening to Karen and Richard Carpenter singing some of my favorite songs of that time. It was great to be able to spend so much time with my brother and sister-in-law. I looked at them as the ideal couple, and romanticized the idea that someday I would have a relationship that would be similar to theirs.

In regards to relationships, Terri really influenced my thinking and my thought process regarding the subject. She shared with me early on that she wasn't planning to have any children. I was disappointed with the news, as I thought Martin would make a wonderful father, but she told me about the birthing process and all of the gory details, and how she just couldn't undergo it, considering all that was involved. I immediately made up my mind that I was never going to have children either. Having children wasn't something that I'd dreamed about as a child anyway, as I was such a tomboy, so it seemed like an easy decision at the time. My sister owned Barbie with a wardrobe of clothes and I had the Ken doll complete with a tuxedo and a swimsuit, but I'd always made fun of May for requesting dolls for Christmas – as I was happy when I got my first baseball mitt and baseball bat.

The description that Terri provided in regards to childbirth sealed the deal for me in my not wanting to have children. I don't know whether it was really the birthing process that scared Terri or the fact that her mother had a physical disease that could have been hereditary, though. Her mother suffered from a rare condition called scleroderma, and it affected her ability to move, as it's a member of the rheumatoid arthritis family. Terri and her sisters cared for their mother, as she wasn't able to undertake her own personal care. Her one sister had no plans to have babies either, as it was often discussed in the dairy mart where we worked. I wondered what my brother thought about not having children, as I'd never really heard him talk about his desire to have a family, but I don't think this had an effect on their relationship; still, I was soon to learn that there was a weak link in their marriage.

I was in my early twenties at the time, and thoughts regarding dating and marriage were entertaining my mind in regards to how my future would look. My role models when it came to relationships were Martin and Terri, but I didn't know that things were not going so well in their personal lives, as neither one of them had indicated to me that they were having problems. I did know that, at one time while working at the dairy mart, my sister-in-law had mentioned that she was attracted to professional-looking men, and I'd found that comment to be odd since it contrasted against my brother, he was such a down to earth electrician. For some reason, that comment remained in my mind – possibly as a subconscious signal as to what was to come.

Being away at college and then in starting my career, I hadn't been as close to their marital situation as I had been previously. It was after my graduation from college and during my first semester as a teacher that things changed. My brother had been working a lot of the midnight shifts at the power plant and Terri was working at the hospital. I wasn't having much success in the dating arena, and Terri was encouraging me to go out to nightclubs in order to meet someone other than the local boys to date.

I thought it odd that she offered to and wanted to go out with me, given that she was a married woman, but I accepted her invites and we'd go to a movie and then stop at some club to have a drink afterwards. Nightclubs were popular at the time, and she usually influenced where we would go. I thought her interest was in helping me to find someone to date, as she was always pointing out attractive men for me. She also attended some of the volleyball games in which I coached also, and she was always looking around the gymnasium for someone who could be a possibility for me to date. She couldn't understand why I hadn't attended the prom in high school or met someone significant to date in college, and I had never shared with her the involvement that I had with Mr. Santini; to my knowledge, she wasn't even aware of his presence in my life. Even though she was close to me, I still didn't feel comfortable revealing my feelings about him to her.

During the spring of 1981, I remember one particular evening that peaked my curiosity about Terri while we were at a nightclub. She was asked to dance by a strange gentleman and, judging by their interaction, I felt as if she knew him. After coming off of the dance floor, she immediately excused herself to go to the lady's room. I was surprised that she'd accepted someone's offer to dance, as she had never done that before. The feelings that came over me as I watched her dance with a strange man were a mixture of annoyance and being peeved that she would dance with someone other than my brother. I sat and waited for her to return from the restroom so that we could talk about it, and after quite a while, I went looking for her and couldn't find her anywhere. It seemed as though she was gone for about forty-five minutes. When she finally did return, I asked her where she'd been and she made up some excuse that she'd only been in the lady's room.

I was so young and naïve at the time that I really did believe her, even though I had looked for her all over the small club without any luck. The thought of her cheating on my brother was not prevalent in my mind, as she just didn't seem like the type. At that time, though, I could not imagine that dancing with someone was anything more than just a dance.

This outing would become significant in my memory, as it would come to mind a few weeks later when my brother had an incident with his motorcycle and landed in the hospital. He had injured one of the lower discs in his back and was going to need an operation. It was during a planned visit to the hospital to see him that Terri and Martin shocked me with some surprising news. It was my brother who told me that they were getting a divorce. As Terri sat silently by his bedside, I stood there in awe – stunned by the announcement that my brother had just made. I hadn't expected for them to ever break up because, in my mind, they were still the perfect couple that I had romanticized. I was shocked by the news, and held my tears back as I questioned them about their decision.

They didn't share with me at the time the reason for their split, but I learned from my brother later on that Terri had met another man at the hospital where she was working, and was planning to move in with him. I immediately wondered how she had met him and what blemish in their marriage had brought about these circumstances, but Terri had never shared with me that she was unhappy, and I'd been unaware of any discord that was creating a rift between she and my brother. I wondered what had caused her to be attracted to someone else to begin with. Was it just the professional aura that she was seeking, and the other man provided that, or was it the close proximity of their work that had brought them close together? I also wondered if my brother had been able to see them drifting apart in their relationship, or if it had been a shock for him when he discovered her infidelity. I had so many questions that loomed in my mind in regards to their relationship; however, I didn't feel comfortable crossing into their personal boundaries. I had respect for their privacy in that regard, though at the same time I wanted to know what blemish had caused their marriage to break.

I especially wondered why Terri wouldn't have shared with me her attraction to someone else, but I guess I truly knew in my mind that that would have been an ultimate betrayal of my brother. In my heart, I knew that it would also have been a confession that would never mend the fence that was now placed between us. Years later, in looking back at our relationship, I know it would have been a struggle for our friendship to continue, even had she shared that secret with me. Had we remained friends, I know in my heart that our relationship would have eventually diminished of its own accord, given the circumstances.

When Martin shared with me that real reason for their divorce, I knew Terri had been using me as her excuse to get out of the house in order to see her lover. I surmised that the evening we'd been at the nightclub was to meet with her new friend; he'd been the one who had asked her to dance and then they'd probably disappeared to his car for a make-out session. I was angry that she would do such a thing to my brother at a time when he was hurting and in pain, and I was also mad that she'd used me as an excuse to see her new friend. I felt as though it was my fault, for having Terri be my accomplice in my search for eligible men to date. I'd given her the excuse to be out of the house, and if it hadn't been for me, she wouldn't have been able to be with him. I carried forth some guilt for being such a good friend to her in that respect.

After seven years of marriage, the announcement about their divorce in a stark hospital room by his bedside came as a shock. My father was also in the room when they told me the news, and he just sat there in silence as they talked with me. I knew that he was there for moral support for my brother, and for me if I needed it. I was in such dismay that I don't think the news sank in at that moment. It was so very hard for me to understand how their relationship was coming to an end. And to top it all off, my sister shared with me later on that I was the last one to find out.

I didn't know it at the time, but this was the last time that I would ever see Terri. She had already made plans to move out of his home. At the hospital, our meeting was brief that day as she told me that it had nothing to do with me, and that she really cared about me and hoped to keep in touch. With tears in her eyes, she gave me a quick hug and goodbye, and then she was on her way. I was feeling such dismay that I don't even remember what my words to her were. I just remember being hurt by the news, and I left the hospital in tears, as I had lost someone who I loved and trusted, but who had betrayed not only my brother, but had used me for her purposes. I never shared my anger about that situation with anyone, and that included my brother, though he might have guessed. It was as though it was something that simply happened, and then we never really talked about it. Her leaving felt as though I'd received the news of a sudden death, and then never really got around to mourning the loss.

Terri's leaving Martin was the first time that I ever witnessed someone just walking away from a relationship. In my mind, a relationship was something that was permanent in spite of all the ups and downs. Up until that point, I had only seen the strong resolve of my father in regards to his commitment to my mother. My image of a romantic marriage had looked like that of what Martin and Terri held together. Their divorce shattered my perception of love and commitment, though, as I now knew that people could literally just walk away without any apparent thought about what was being left behind. The dissolving of their marriage was a rude awakening for me, and it did cause some confusion in my understanding of love and commitment. It made me question the word "trust", and how you would recognize someone who you could truly trust.

It also made me wonder about my future relationships, in regards to love and men, and if I would ever have a stable commitment. I wondered if I would ever walk away from anyone, or if someone would walk away from me. I also knew that I didn't want someone to remain with me out of pity or if they no longer loved me, which further complicated things, but I prayed that if someone needed to walk away from me, it would not be when I needed them the most. I could not imagine why Terri had chosen such a time to make the break from Martin, and why she couldn't have waited until he was out of the hospital. I'm sure that it had been discussed prior to that event because I can't believe that she was so cold-hearted in that regard.

In spite of all of this, of course, Martin was still in the hospital and still facing an operation. I determined that I would support him and help see him through his difficult time. After my brother had his operation on his disc and returned to his home, I moved in with him for a short period of time. He needed someone to help him out around the house, as well as tend to his yard and garden.

During our time together, Terri showed up one day while I was at school teaching. The purpose of her visit was to ask my brother if she could come back. He was so hurt that she'd cheated on him that he wouldn't give her another chance; the mark that she had left on him was deep enough that he wasn't able to forgive her, and so the divorce became finalized. When I questioned his actions, I finally learned the reason for their divorce. He shared with me how she'd cheated on him with another man and that was too painful.

I stayed with my brother till the end of my school term, as he needed my care. We got along well together, except in that his only complaint was that I walked heavily across his hardwood floors in my shoes and boots, and this annoyed him. Regardless of my brother's complaints, though, I was happy to be able to assist him at a time when he needed it most.

This occasion would not be the only time that I would live with Martin to care for him, though. Prior to my finding my first apartment in 1984, I moved in with him to help him for a short period of time while my parents were in Florida. He was working a lot of overtime at the plant, and I was doing my substitute teaching and in need of some extra income. He helped me out by letting me live with him, and in return I cooked and cleaned and took care of the yard. I was grateful to be out of my family home and to have some independence to come and go as I pleased.

We didn't know it at the time, but it turned out to be a timely visit. One evening, after working the evening shift, Martin came home having terrible abdominal pains in his bowel area. I was fast asleep, and he woke me up to ask me to take him to the emergency room. I immediately got dressed and got him into my low-riding car that I had at the time, and unfortunately it served to give him a quick and uncomfortable ride to the hospital. He felt every bump in the road on the forty-five-minute ride to the hospital; that was an important drive, though, painful as it was. We didn't know it, but his bowel was in danger of rupturing and his life was in immediate danger. Once we got to the emergency room, the doctor took him immediately into surgery. He had a severe case of diverticulitis that was causing the pain and needed to have some of his bowel removed.

It was a serious operation, and the doctor said that, had he waited another hour, he would have died. I sat through the night alone, waiting for him to come out of the surgery. I remember praying frantically for his safety during surgery, and for a speedy recovery. I worried that he was going to die on the operating table and that I would never see him again, and I felt helpless and all alone as I sat and waited for any news. My sister had small children at home and wasn't able to leave them to come to the hospital, though I don't know where my brother William was, as he was often unavailable during family events of any type, emergency or otherwise.

Martin spent several long weeks recovering in the hospital, and then returned back to his home with a reversible colostomy bag. He had an extensive recovery period at home, and I helped him tend to his personal care needs that included cleaning and replacing his bag on a daily basis. My brother faints at the sight of blood, and I have an extra sensitive sense of smell and react badly to anything with a strong odor, but between the two of us we managed to get his bag situated. I tended to the house and helped him as much as I possibly could, as he was bedridden. Several months later, he went back into the hospital to have the colostomy bag removed and to have his bowel resection. It was another major operation and he spent most of the recovery time in the hospital. I was just grateful that he had a full recovery, though, and that the bag would not be a permanent part of his life.

My brother's journey after his divorce was physically challenging, and I sometimes wonder if his divorce was the cause of his physical ailments. Yet, I was proud of his strong rebuilding of his life and that he kept a strong faith in having a great future ahead of him; I admired his ability to overcome a serious illness, as well as a difficult emotional time. In hindsight, I think that observing my brother during the rough path that he travelled helped me to have the same type of inner resolve during my own troublesome periods in life as I moved forward from that point.

My brother and I became very close during this period, as we were both mourning the loss of someone whom we'd thought of as being special, only to be disappointed in their actions. My brother handled his situation well, and was able to rise above his difficulties. I was only happy that we had each other to lean on for support

The imperfection that my brother received as a result of his marriage to Terri was not only an emotional blemish, but one that left a mark on his physical health. The unseen stress took its toll and left a flaw inside his body. I often wonder if he may have gotten sick from harboring negative feelings about his marriage. Either way, I knew that my brother's heart and soul now had a blemish, and that his physical body now had one, as well. I wondered if he'd completely healed, or if it would stay with him for the rest of his life. I also knew that, somewhere along the line, Terri had also received a blemish that had caused her to do what she did. And I knew that she and my brother had created a blemish together. It made me question how many blemishes one could have before they would actually break.

The flaw that Terri had left in regards to my own life was not a physical flaw, but one that made its mark instantaneously. Her departure from my life was utterly hurtful at the time, the announcement of their divorce came as a such a shock. Years later, as I write these words, another dent has marked my heart as I've recalled this time in my life – the realization of how sometimes it is a survival mechanism, to hide your true feelings, only to have them resurface years later. I didn't properly mourn the loss of our friendship at that time, as I needed to be strong and carry on with my life, and to tend to my brother. I put all of these feelings that I had on the back burner, and only gave them their proper burial as I wrote this chapter. The emotions that welled up inside of me were surprising, even these many years later, because it was as though it had all just happened yesterday. I finally feel as though I have given the loss of that friendship a proper mourning, though, and as if I have healed the bruise that it made such a long time ago.

After my brother made his recovery, he treated me to a week at Myrtle Beach that we spent together. I drove my car and we enjoyed some wonderful carefree time. We both needed the time away and, upon our return, I moved into my first apartment. It was at that time when I signed us up for some ballroom dance classes. It was my attempt to get my brother out of the house and socializing again.

My brother didn't meet anyone to date in the dance classes, and I really don't think that he was in too big of a hurry to meet anyone at all. Unfortunately, his troubles with women did not end with Terri, and I was soon aware that he had more blemishes in the making. Several years later, he married another woman named Carol. His marriage to her is probably not even worth mentioning, as it only lasted thirty days. Strangely, she was mentally imbalanced and took to locking herself in the bathroom on a regular basis. One day, my brother arrived home to an empty house and an empty bank account; understandably, it was after that that my brother had a slight change in personality.

The warm and easy-going brother who I'd known so well became a little more hardened to the ways of the world. In my estimation, he became a little more cautious about who he would trust. It wasn't that he was not so likeable, but that he wasn't going to let anyone take advantage of his kind nature anymore. He was learning some of the cruel lessons that the world has to offer. I didn't blame him for his change of heart and, in some respects, I wish that I could have been more like him in that way. He seemed to put up a wall that was in stark contrast to the brother that I'd once known. Inside, I knew that he was still the same kind, warm man who I loved in spite of it all. I knew that the blemishes that he had received had reached the limits he could tolerate. I didn't know what the outcome might be on his physical health, if they exceeded those limits, but I wondered if his body would break. I didn't worry so much about his emotional well-being, as he had proved to me that he was mentally strong and could endure the hard knocks life could hand out.

As a result of his troubles with women and my own troubles with men, we would spend a lot of time with our parents on the weekends – playing golf, going to dinner, and just enjoying family time. Martin and I would also vacation with our parents in Florida, and be able to have a lot of fun times together through the years. It would take both of us a long time to meet our current marriage partners, and these years weren't without a lot of bumps in the road.

And so, having Terri in my life was a great joy, but also a great disappointment. I cared about her and, in my heart, I have been able to forgive her – as she had to do what she needed to do to make herself happy. I have learned that we cannot control the actions of others; we can only be responsible for our own actions. I am sure, in retrospect, that she may have felt bad in leaving my brother the way that she did.

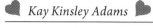
Over the years, I can only hope that she may have given me a thought every now and again.

On the whole, though, I am grateful that she was present in my life for my important years as a teenager and throughout college. It was nice to have someone who was like a big sister to me and who at times gave me the guidance that I really needed from my mother. Her absence left a mark on my heart, as her leaving felt as though I was being abandoned, and so much so that I wished that we would have been able to stay in touch... but it probably would have made things difficult between myself and my brother. Things would have never been the same between us, as the trust I had in her was destroyed. As painful as it was to lose someone so close to me, God made the right choice as to whom I should keep in my life and who should be discarded, as I am forever grateful to have a big brother who has been a strong guiding force in my life.

Danielle & Dennis – 1985

Once in a blue moon, you meet someone who you know you were destined to meet. In the summer of 1985, instead of meeting just one such person, I met two people in instances that I felt were very serendipitous.

Up until this point, men had been so prominent in my life that I'd had yet to meet a woman who would play such a huge role. When I met Danielle, of course, I didn't know that she would become so important to me, but I knew right away that she was different than most other women I had ever met. She was sparkling with personality and her eyes had an intensity that could pull you in from across the room with their brightness. She had a unique quality to her voice also, and could make a sarcastic comment under her breath and then follow it with her own laugh, but in a way that was likeable. Sometimes, I would have to listen carefully when she spoke or I would lose my place in her conversations. Danielle's tireless energy and chatter could be endless, and one would wonder how someone could have so much to say. Regardless, I found it all to be very endearing.

It was in a small community college dance class where I met Danielle and her husband, Neil, who had accompanied her. Neil was very easy-going and was a great partner for Danielle. His sense of humor helped to make the class enjoyable by entertaining us with his quick wit.

My brother, Martin, was my companion, as he had recovered from back surgery and a divorce from his wife of seven years. I was concerned about his social life, so I'd signed us both up for the ballroom dance class – as I was determined to get him back in the swing of things! I don't know what I was thinking, really, as our genes had not given either one of us an ounce of rhythm.

Nevertheless, we were faithful to our weekly dance instruction, and there we met Neil and Danielle. We became friendly and, after class, we would go out for a bite to eat or out to a nightclub to practice some of our dance steps on a real dance floor. It was the 80s, after all, and dancing was all the craze. At that time, nightclubs were filled with people listening to Madonna, doing the electric slide, and attempting the famous Michael Jackson moonwalk.

My friendship with Danielle escalated quickly, and before I knew it we were constant companions. I had just moved into my first studio apartment at this point, and it was only a few minutes from Danielle's home. She immediately took me under her wing and had me over to her home for dinner. We would go out to lunch often, and just sit and talk as we got to know each other. I felt like I'd met a female soulmate, we enjoyed so many of the same things. We even went to the same gym and took aerobic dance classes together.

Dancing became something that we both enjoyed, and it almost became an obsession for the two of us. Danielle and Neil had three small boys who were close in age and she often referred to our dancing as her way of releasing the stresses of her daily routine and taking care of that family. We also went out to the nightclubs as a pair and spent our evenings dancing with whoever we could find to dance with, or the majority of the time we would just dance with each other. At the end of the evening, we would sit in her car in front of her home and have some very deep discussions about everything. After a few months of being friends, there wasn't too much that we didn't know about each other.

I shared my deepest secrets with her – about my mother, and about the relationships that I'd had with men. For some reason, it seemed easy to talk with her, as she seemed to understand me and, after such a short period of time, to care about me. She offered her opinions as to how to deal with the remnants of the past, and I appreciated her for her care and concern, and I listened to her and to

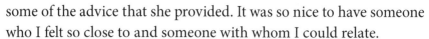

some of the advice that she provided. It was so nice to have someone who I felt so close to and someone with whom I could relate.

Danielle was about six years older than myself, but she at times treated me like her daughter. I didn't mind that she lectured me about my eating habits or gave me ideas on how to look and dress professionally. She boosted my confidence and helped me to see that I had a lot to offer, despite the fact that I was lacking confidence in myself at that time. I had been beating myself up about the poor decisions I had made, and it was reflected in my sense of self. She boosted my confidence, though, by constantly telling me how attractive I was and how successful that I could be if I put my mind to it. Being around her was easy because she made me feel so good about myself.

When I met Danielle, I had been disappointed by a lot of people and I was afraid to care too much, for fear of getting hurt. I didn't know what to expect from friendship or, actually, how to even be a friend. It was something that I was learning about anew, and I was trying to be a good friend in return for what she offered me. The one thing that I did know was that she cared about me and did not judge me for my past behavior, or for being a product of a mother with a mental illness.

Looking back, I hope that I provided the same type of support to her that she needed, as her personal life was being tested. I know that I was her accomplice in providing the escape that she needed from her home life, at least. She was in the midst of caring for her husband and three young boys, and at times felt that it was a difficult task. As dancing had become her therapy, I sometimes wondered if her husband resented me for the distraction that I provided to her. He joined us at the dance clubs occasionally, and he didn't seem to mind, but one never knows what goes on behind closed doors. I didn't want to be a wedge in what seemed like a good marriage between two people who enjoyed each other's company, though.

At the time, Danielle also enjoyed going to nightclubs where male strippers performed. The Chippendales were a popular touring dance troupe at the time, and they entertained women by dressing in costumes, presenting themselves in roles such as policemen and firemen, and would finish their act by stripping down to their g-strings. We would drive great distances to follow certain performers that she felt were top notch! It was unbelievable how many women attended these events and went wild over their antics. Danielle introduced me to this scene, and I'd go with her even though it wasn't my favorite type of entertainment – it reminded me too much of the time that Mickey had taken me to a strip club. Even though it was not my cup of tea, though, I went with her, as I really cared about her. My friendship with Danielle was delightful to say the least, as she entertained me with her great sense of humor and she taught me how to laugh again. Laughter had too often seemed to be missing from my life, and she taught me how to go out and have some innocent fun.

One evening, while out at a nightclub celebrating my twenty-seventh birthday, it was Danielle who introduced me to the other person who I ended up feeling was something more than a chance encounter in my life. His name was Dennis, and he just happened to be her children's dentist whom she had known for a few years. Ironically, he had asked me to dance earlier in the evening and I had brushed him off. While I'd been exiting the dance floor at one point, he'd offered the invitation; and when I refused, he said, "But I am a dentist." I thought that was a strange comment to make at the time, as I really didn't care who he was. Nevertheless, after our formal introduction, he asked me out on a date for the following day. I wasn't really in the mood to date anyone; I just didn't want to be bothered. It was with some urging from Danielle that I accepted his offer to play golf the next day. Later on, I found out that she'd had a little crush on Dennis herself, and wanted to know more about him. She wasn't interested in having an affair with him, but wanted to live through me vicariously.

Dennis, as obvious from his declaration, was very proud of his profession and had a lot of confidence. He was tall, had an athletic build, and had striking blue eyes. He was approximately forty years old at the time when we met and had been married before. He had two boys that were eight years old and twelve, and he had joint custody of them, alternating custody with his ex-wife on a bi-weekly basis. After I'd gotten to know him a bit, he would refer to his ex-wife as a tumor. At the time, I thought that was fairly odd terminology to use in reference to someone that he'd once been married to, but I didn't question him about it.

After our first date on the golf course, we became regular golf partners and would see other several times a week. I had a lot of freedom, as I was working at odd jobs to meet my expenses for the studio apartment that I had moved into. Since my departure from teaching, I had taken on a waitressing job at one of the nightclubs Danielle and I frequented, and I worked a few evenings a week there since I had basically thrown my teaching career out the window. I'd decided to pursue other opportunities, but it was not going all that well, as the job market was limited. However, I was also studying to get my licenses to sell insurance, mutual funds, and annuities, as I wanted to pursue a job in the investment world. To help supplement the income from my waitressing job, I also cleaned house, mowed yards, and did other little odd jobs to pay for my modest rent.

The small studio apartment that I now lived in was, strangely, situated midway between the homes of Danielle and Dennis. It was a three-room apartment on the third floor of an old red brick home in a small town not far from my family home, and it was about a forty-five-minute ride to my parents' home. It was shabbily furnished with a bedroom set that my brother Martin had given to me, along with a bright orange sofa. My mother had donated an old kitchen table and chair set from her collection of wares in the basement, and May had given me some kitchenware to outfit the kitchen. I'd purchased the remaining items from flea markets and the local thrift store, and I was happy with my living space, pleased to be independent even though I wasn't making much money at the time. Somehow, I was able to manage to pay my rent and expenses. I had high hopes for the future also, and I felt sure that someday I was going to be successful.

Dennis didn't think much of my place and made fun of my situation. Not long into our relationship, he started to tell me that I wasn't very successful and that the career path I was choosing wasn't a good one. I ignored his bad remarks and, not having much experience in actually dating, I held my thoughts to myself. These comments of course hurt my feelings because I knew that I had the willpower and determination to become whatever I wanted to become. Regardless of what he thought, I continued to study for my licenses and get any work that I could muster up.

After our first date, truth be told, I had become quite infatuated with Dennis, as I was attracted to his good looks and confident manner. We'd immediately started to spend every moment with each other, and that gave me the impression that he felt the same way I did. It wasn't long into the relationship before we became intimate either, as I imagined that we were soulmates in regards to our compatibility. I almost became obsessed with the thought that he was going to be the man who I was going to marry, as it wasn't very often that I met someone who enjoyed all the sporting activities that I enjoyed and who I was physically attracted to.

Thinking back, I can say now that it was probably due to my lack of experience that I didn't consider other compatibility issues. I'm now appalled to think how I made myself so very available to his requests for my time. After the initial burst of dating, Dennis became inconsistent in his pursuing me, as he would call me only at the last minute to go play golf, tennis, go to the movies, or just hang out. In my eyes, everything seemed to be going well, as I had met his children and we had gone on a long weekend getaway together over the fourth of July. He'd even invited me to go on a trip to Haiti for the following January, though I didn't have the funds to go and had to refuse since he wanted me to pay my own way.

Meanwhile, I would confer with Danielle on a regular basis about our dates, as she wanted to hear all of the details. Danielle warned me not to make myself so readily available to him and I justified it by saying that he would always call me, and not just when I was expecting to be called. She shared with me that I needed to play my cards differently if he was the one who I really wanted to marry; her advice was that I not make myself so readily available, as it wasn't challenging enough for someone like Dennis. In my mind, I really didn't feel that I needed to play such games. Danielle was very intuitive, though, and I now know that she was right in making her judgments about his personality and the dynamics of our relationship at the time. However, had I listened to her, it probably wouldn't have changed the outcome, as I feel he was placed in my life so that I could learn a hard lesson.

I still had plenty of time to spend with Danielle, but I would spend a lot of my time waiting for Dennis to call me. In spite of Danielle's advice and her attempts to distract me, sometimes I would cut my trips to visit her or my parents short since I couldn't wait to get home and check my answering machine for a missed call. In hindsight, I can't believe how much time I wasted with just waiting for him to call me. Had I gotten myself involved in an activity to keep my mind occupied, I may not have gotten so obsessed with him. My father urged me to donate any extra time I had to the hospital as a candy striper; I think he knew that I was moonstruck over someone who didn't deserve to have my time, as he could surely see a change in my behavior.

My parents hadn't met Dennis, but what little they knew about him didn't seem to bode well – at least in their eyes. They wondered why they hadn't met him if he was of such importance to me. I hadn't told him about my mother, though, and so I hadn't yet extended an invitation for him to meet my parents. It wasn't that I didn't want him to meet them, but in retrospect, I also realize that he showed no interest in wanting to meet them. This should have been a clear warning sign to me that he really didn't care that much about me. What would happen next would increase their dislike for him, even prior to their ever meeting him.

I'm sorry to say that it after only a few dates with Dennis that I quickly became physically intimate with him. Considering some of my past mistakes, I'd thought that I would wait to get to know someone prior to moving a relationship to a sexual level; however, things didn't happen that way, and I found myself in a physical relationship without my having really taken the time to get to know him. If I had it all to do over again, things would be quite different. As it was, though, I let my physical attraction to him guide my instincts, and I landed in a predicament as a result. I had started dating Dennis in late June of 1985, and by late August of the same year I discovered that I was pregnant. I had been experimenting with birth control pills, as I found the first type I'd tried made me ill, and I had missed a period. It was Dennis who suggested that I get an in-home pregnancy test kit, as he seemed to know the exact moment that it happened. He later shared with me that, because of his age, he hadn't thought that he could still make anyone pregnant, and he'd been curious if he could still father a child. My reaction to this was surprisingly calm, and I didn't say anything in regards to that intentional injustice. Looking back, I can't believe that I wasn't outraged at his declaration, and that I instead handled the news as though it was an everyday statement that one might make. I guess that I thought that everything would be okay, and I really wasn't thinking about the ramifications that this would have on my life.

In the same conversation as that revealing remark, he made another admission that I found distasteful, in the fact that he and his ex-wife had used abortion as their birth control. This wasn't how I'd been brought up, certainly, and the ethics of abortion really didn't fit in with my moral code. Once again, though, I just let that comment slip by without any rebuttal. I think at the time that I was so smitten with him that I was afraid that, if I expressed my real thoughts, he would not love me. I wanted so badly to be loved by someone that I was afraid to speak out in regards to my own beliefs. I think my silence confirmed to him that I was in agreement with him and his way of thinking, but little did he know that I was simmering with anger internally. I cannot believe that I let these comments be said to me without any disagreement in return. I know that my self-confidence had to be at an all -time low in order for me to let such a difference of opinion pass me by.

Once my pregnancy was confirmed, Dennis was very matter of fact in telling me that I needed to get an abortion. He told me that he would be emotionally and financially supportive, but that he was not going to marry me. It was only at this point that I confided with him that I did not believe in abortion, and that I wouldn't be having one. He attempted to encourage me by telling me that "no one would want to marry a single mom." This infuriated me, as I didn't believe it to be true; however, I let that comment slide by without a rebuttal, as well. After he would make such comments, there was a deafening silence, as I didn't want to get in an argument with him. I think I felt that he was better than me because of his standing in life, and because of his attempts to belittle me. He continually made it clear to me that I wasn't going to be successful in any efforts that I made to better myself. This was such a stark contrast to my relationship with Danielle, as she only saw the best in me and what I had to offer.

Danielle was very disturbed by the news of my pregnancy, and she actually threatened to call him on my behalf. She was also angered by his reaction to the pregnancy and by the behaviors that we were both exhibiting, and continued to give me advice about how to handle my situation... but I was fearful of losing my relationship with Dennis as a result. Her moral code was in alignment with mine, though, and she was very supportive of my not having an abortion.

After the initial discussion with Dennis regarding my pregnancy, and his urging me to have an abortion, we would sporadically see each other for the next month – but with little discussion of the proverbial elephant in the room, as neither one of us brought up the topic. Finally, one day he called and invited me out to a Saturday evening dinner so that we could have a conversation about our circumstances. From the tone of his voice on the phone, I thought he had maybe changed his view, as he was being very sweet. I looked forward to the evening, as I was encouraged by the thought that he may have changed his mind; in my mind, I was hopeful that he really did love me and that he wanted to father my baby. I even thought that maybe he would offer a possible marriage proposal.

That Saturday evening, he picked me up at my apartment; I'd dressed and prepared myself for a possible romantic interlude. Danielle, on the other hand, had warned me not to get my hopes up and to think things through very carefully. She was the voice of reason, in that she doubted he was going to propose a marriage.

The evening started out with a feeling of great anticipation, as he had taken me to a very nice place for dinner. However, the evening ended in disappointment when the conversation turned into him trying to convince me once again to have an abortion. He repeated the previous conversation and became more adamant in regards to nobody ever wanting to marry a single mom. Secretly, I wondered how someone could be so cruel as to say such a thing to someone who was carrying his baby. Once again, I didn't have the nerve to speak back regarding what I was really feeling inside. I just let him dictate to me what his wishes were in comparison to mine.

When I left that evening, he was very direct in giving me a date and time for the following week, for when he planned to pick me up for the procedure. I didn't give him any indication that I was a willing candidate and would be following his guidance, and it was with great distress that I went home and cried about my situation. In my heart, I also knew that it was time that I told my parents, as I knew that they were going to be very disappointed in me. I had only shared the news with Danielle immediately, and she had been the one who'd started mothering me about the care that I needed to take in regards to my pregnancy.

It was after that dinner that I became very concerned about the future of myself and my baby, as I wasn't sure how we were going to manage. The realization that I was going to be a single mom finally started to settle in. Over the past month, I had been studying hard to pass my exams to become a licensed sales representative who could sell investments. It gave me some peace of mind to know that I had been successful in achieving my goals in that respect, at least, as I had obtained my licenses and been pursuing opportunities to find work locally by passing out resumes to prospective employers. In frustration, I had taken a job as an assistant to a contractor, and was painting the outside and inside of homes. I wasn't fond of climbing up and down tall ladders with a bucket of paint or fighting with wallpaper on rainy days, but I was getting a little more money. I knew that I wasn't going to be able to continue with that type of job once my pregnancy became more apparent, and I was also worried about the smell of the paint and whether it would have an effect on my unborn child.

Dennis had actually made me feel ashamed that I'd accepted such a position, and felt it was beneath him to be dating someone who did that type of work. With this being said, though, he had asked me to clean his home – which I did on a weekly basis, as well. Against the advice of Danielle, I'd accepted the job in addition to the other petty jobs I was doing. I knew I was a good housecleaner and that I did an exceptional job, as I was obsessive in that regard. I had lots of experience from my upbringing, but no matter how great a job I did, it was never good enough for him. He would routinely pick at some small detail that was insignificant and make it into a major criticism. He also told me on a regular basis that he liked to see women dressed in professional outfits, such as suits. The stinging comments about my lack of a good job and desirable profession were consistent, and lacking in foresight. I had faith that I would achieve the results that I wanted, as I had a lot of determination and I was making every attempt to get a job by passing out my resumes and filling out applications for employment, but things were moving slowly.

With my lack of good employment and no reward for my efforts, I was starting to feel beaten down. I wondered what was to become of me and my unborn child. I had no doubt in my mind that I was going to do a good job in taking care of the baby, though, regardless of whether or not it had a father. I simply had such strong feelings for Dennis that I was blind to what the future might have been like with him in my life. I knew that we had some differences in regards to having children, even though it wasn't something I had imagined for myself. I'd really never planned on having children, as I knew I was selfish in wanting to always have the freedom to go and do as I pleased. With that being said, I was willing to adapt to the situation and do the best I could to be a good mother, regardless of my selfishness.

It was a very traumatic time for me, as my belief system obviously didn't coincide with his, and I was being tested. I finally shared with my parents that I was pregnant, though, and as I'd suspected, they were disappointed. My sister May was excited to learn that her son was going to have a playmate, at least; she was truly happy for me, but felt sorry for my situation.

Meanwhile, my parents questioned me about how I was going to support the child that I was planning to have – and they made it clear that they would not be the childcare team. They continued to question me about all of the dreams and goals that I'd shared with them in regards to my future, and also as to how I was going to carry them out while being a single mom. Through all of the ongoing conversations, they never told me to get an abortion, but they did formulate some sort of a plan.

The day after my Saturday evening dinner with Dennis, I went to my parents' home for a Sunday lunch. My brother Martin was in attendance and that gave me a lot of comfort, as I didn't expect what happened next. During lunch, my mother told me about some old wives' tales in regards to the loss of unexpected pregnancies. One was to go horseback riding, with the thought that it would jar the fetus loose from the womb, and the other tale was that one could douche with Coca-Cola. I had never heard of either tale, and just took the conversation with a grain of salt.

Well, after lunch on this particular Sunday, my father suggested a Sunday drive, which we had not done in years. He had us all pile into the car and we went driving along a number of very bumpy country roads with lots of dirt. Some of them, I hadn't even known existed, and my brother Martin and I were flying around in the back seat. My father was driving too fast for the road conditions as he silently smoked on his pipe. He let the heavy stream of pipe smoke escape through the driver's window, as it was a beautiful fall day. They never told me that their intentions were for me to lose the baby, but halfway through the car ride, that is what I suspected. At the end of the day, I went home and cried some more, as I was so disappointed in myself for having gotten myself into such a predicament. I knew that my parents expected great things from me, and I'd let them down.

Dennis had set the date of the procedure for that coming Wednesday, and he was planning to pick me up. I spent the next two days after that visit to my parents just worrying about what I was going to do, though. I did a lot of praying, and some feeling sorry for myself. That Tuesday evening in late October, I went to bed very distraught and with tears in my eyes, knowing that an abortion was not the right thing for me to do. In the middle of the night, I was startled awake by the sound of a woman's voice. I felt a presence in my room and heard her say, "Not to worry – everything is going to be alright." I didn't know if I was dreaming or if there really was an apparition in my apartment that evening. It seemed so real to me, as I was overcome with the knowledge that, in the morning, I had to get up early and leave my apartment prior to the arrival of Dennis.

The next morning, I got up with great haste and left my apartment without leaving any sign in regards to my disappearance. I decided that I would go spend the day with my mother and my sister, as I needed to be comforted. I drove out to their home and sat with them all day, just talking and visiting with them. About three o'clock in the afternoon, I started to bleed lightly and became concerned; I didn't know what was happening. My sister had the foresight to suggest that I lie down for a little bit and put my legs up. I took her advice and then decided after an hour or so that I needed to go home, as I felt that something wasn't right.

By the time I arrived home, I was bleeding quite heavily and experiencing small contractions, and I wasn't sure what to do. I called Danielle and she came rushing over to my aid. She quickly determined that she needed to take me to the emergency room of the hospital. We both felt that it was possible that I was going to miscarriage the baby. My experience at the emergency room was mortifying as I answered some embarrassing questions about the nature of my pregnancy and the father of my baby. I was then immediately placed in a stark room with a bed that was surrounded by curtains. They placed an IV in my arm and left me alone, only to check on me periodically. The nurse also indicated to me that I might have a miscarriage. I wasn't exactly sure what was going to happen, but I was very nervous. My cramping had become more intense, offering a strong feeling that I was going to have a baby.

Danielle was with me through the entire time, and only left my side to go make a phone call to Dennis to let him know where I was and what was happening. After several long hours of discomfort and no apparent loss of my child, the hospital sent me home. Danielle didn't seem happy about the phone conversation that she'd had with Dennis, but she didn't share all of the details with me, either. The only thing that she told me was that he'd said "It's a blessing in disguise." Regardless of that statement, I kept wondering – all through the hours of discomfort – when he was going to show up at the hospital. I was happy that Danielle was there to support me through that terrible time, but I was sad that Dennis never showed.

Danielle drove me home after stopping at the pharmacy to pick up some medication, as I was still having painful cramping in my abdomen. She assisted me up the three flights to my studio apartment and, to both our amazement, I lost the baby at the top of the steps. I was very traumatized, reacting to how it had happened, so expectantly and so quickly. I was so very grateful that Danielle was there and had the presence of mind to know how to help me. She immediately pulled the mattress off of my bed and helped me onto the floor so that I could be comfortable, and she spent the evening laying on the floor with me while I had uncontrollable bouts of weeping. Danielle did everything that a mother would do to comfort a child who had been though a terrible ordeal; she made me tea and talked with me about how I would get through it, and promised me that things would be better. I could not have asked for a more caring person to have helped me in such an awkward time. Danielle called Dennis once again to let him know of the loss, and she also called my parents to let them know that I was alright. She spent the night with me, though she needed to leave early in the morning to get her children off to school. I will be forever grateful to her for the kindness that she showed me at that time in my life.

First thing in the morning, Dennis called me – but only to tell me directly that "it was a blessing in disguise." He also told me once again that I would have had a difficult time finding a man to marry me as a single mom. I listened as he said these unkind things to me, and I listened in silence. Our conversation was very short and to the point, with no other words to best describe it. Danielle had left prior to the call, and I was now all alone – left to sob even more on the floor of my apartment. I really don't know what I would have done without Danielle.

A few hours later, my parents arrived to visit with me. They told me that they were sorry for how things had happened and for the outcome, but also told me that it was probably for the best. I really didn't have much to say, as I was so heartbroken and so embarrassed for my parents to see me in such a bad way. They offered to make me some food, but I really wasn't hungry, and there was a lot of silence as they sat and stared at me. I know that they loved me and wanted to help me, but they just weren't sure what they could do or say to make things better. I'd never had such an awkward moment with my parents as I did at that time, as they had never seen me in such despair; the tears that I cried on that particular day were for the loss of a child that I would never see, and for the knowledge that a man who I loved did not love me in return.

I was heartbroken that Dennis would treat me with such a lack of care when I cared so much, and I could not believe the words that he had spoken to me in regards to the loss of our child. I was sorry for the loss of my unborn baby, as well, as I knew that I would have been a good mother, even if I could accept that I was not in a good place financially or mature enough to have a child – still, I acknowledged to myself that I would have loved it with all of my heart. I also knew that I would have done anything to give it a good life, regardless of not having a father present. Looking back, I guess that I was hoping that things could work out in our relationship, and that Dennis would change his mind once the child was born.

I spent the next few days recovering in my apartment, having crying spells off and on. I didn't do much, as I was still laying on my mattress on the floor. I don't even remember eating or drinking much during those days. I kept playing out the scenario with Dennis over and over again in my mind, and trying to fix my thoughts on my future. I understood that I needed to get myself back up on my feet and turn myself in a new direction, and during those few days of my despair, I formulated a new plan to be what I wanted to be. Once again, I needed to escape my situation by starting over somewhere else, and I was going to show Dennis that I could be successful; I was determined that I was going to become a professional. My only hope was to make use of the licenses that I had obtained to sell investments. With great fervor, I decided that I would drive to a larger city sixty miles away, and distribute my resumes there since I was having no success locally.

The following week, I got dressed in my professional attire and armed myself with a ton of resumes. Each morning, I drove an hour into the city, parked my car, and went from building to building on foot as I knocked on doors seeking gainful employment. With a map in hand, I spent every day for a week searching the strange town for work. I was a bit familiar with the city, as I had a friend from college who lived close by and I had spent time at her home; it had been during those visits that we would visit the seemingly large city. Now, I used that bit of knowledge and then went home each night – exhausted, yet hopeful that something would pan out as a result of my efforts.

In the meantime, I had received a letter from Dennis in the mail, telling me that I was too inexperienced in the ways of the world and that I needed to basically find myself. He wanted to remain friends and to leave the door open for the future. It was a strange letter, as he was telling me on one hand that he wanted me to move on, but also that he didn't want me to. This letter sent me spiraling into a bout of depression, as I had not seen or spoke to him since the loss of the baby, and I was working so hard toward my goals, but without any success.

The receipt of the letter sent me into another crying spell that was pretty intense. At one point, I went into my kitchen and picked up a knife and aimed at my heart. I wanted to end my own life, as I was tired of the disappointments and the let-downs. I couldn't understand what I had done wrong, to be so deserving of such treatment, as I thought of myself as a good person and I couldn't understand why the world was treating me so poorly. I wanted so badly to end my misery and to be rid of myself. I had a lot of anger about my life in general at that point, and I didn't know what to do with all of the feelings that I was having. In my despair and in a flood of tears, I knew that I was not able to pull off the mission that I wanted to accomplish. As much as I wanted to, I would not let myself drive the knife into my heart, or slit my wrists, for that matter. In my soul, I knew that it was the wrong thing to do and that God had a better plan for me. I also knew that it was an ultimate sin to take your own life, and that no person was worth that. I couldn't give up my faith and my hope in spite of the difficulty of the journey I was on. So, I put the knife down and went into my bedroom and prayed that the night would end, and that the universe would relent in my favor. I asked God a lot of questions that particular evening, and I prayed that He would restore peace to my heart and my soul. The evening was one of the most difficult evenings that I had ever endured, as all of the heaviness of the previous weeks had come tumbling toward this pivotal point.

Getting up the next morning, I knew that I had a problem, and yet I wasn't really sure how to fix it. Through the previous weeks, a thought had been formulating that I needed to have some help in fixing myself, as I kept asking myself what was wrong with me. Danielle had been there for me, but that didn't seem to be enough and I needed something more. I was searching for answers as to why I was continually getting myself into situations that were not good for me.

In thinking about how to get help, I decided to go over to the mental ward to which my mother had been admitted on so many occasions. I decided that it was time for me to go and admit myself, as I had big problems that I could not seem to resolve, and I thought that maybe I had a mental problem which couldn't be solved through only my own efforts. I was feeling so sad and depressed, and finally got up enough nerve to walk into the place in an attempt to sign myself in. I knew that I really needed to talk with someone, and yet I was so very nervous. After waiting with trepidation for what seemed like an hour, I was finally escorted back to the office of a psychologist. I surprised myself, in that I actually stayed to sit down and didn't just decide to dart out the door at the last moment.

I met the doctor that was sitting behind a large desk in his office, and he looked at me over the top of his big thick black glasses as I entered the room. He appeared to be in his mid-fifties and looked at me with a knowing stare. He asked me why I was interested in signing myself into the mental ward, and I gave him a fifteen-minute, non-stop dissertation of my recent life's events, but purposely excluded the fact that I'd recently wanted to kill myself. To add to the fury of my words, I tossed in that my mother was mentally ill and that he might know her, as she'd been a guest in their facility from time to time.

He offered what I felt was a very quick assessment of the situation, as he told me that I did not have my mother's illness and that I was just learning some very hard facts about life. His reasoning in regard to my mother's illness was that I would have shown signs and symptoms long before the present moment. That knowledge alone actually sent a great relief through me, as it was something that I had long wondered about. In an authoritative manner, he then proceeded to tell me that I was responsible for the decisions that I had made in my life and, as a result, had simply landed myself in some difficult predicaments for someone my age. He also told me that, based on the manner in which I'd strode into the room, he could tell from the way my boots hit the ground that I was a very angry young lady. He suggested that I find some way to deal with that anger, and also find out what the source of it was. His conclusion was that I needed to make better decisions in regards to my relationships, and the result would be better outcomes.

I exited his office and felt a sigh of relief in knowing that I didn't need to be admitted, and that I wasn't mentally ill. I walked out of his office with a new awareness about myself; I'd known that I was angry, but I was surprised at such a quick assessment in that regard. I also knew that I needed to work on releasing that anger, or it could destroy me, and his comments allowed me to notice that I did walk hard, digging my boot heels into the ground. When I arrived home, I looked at the bottom of my boots and the shoes that I owned, and took notice of the worn heels that had been ground down as a result of my hard steps. When I walked, I determined that I'd try to walk more lightly and to not make such a hard-sounding noise with my shoes, as I thought that maybe if I walked lightly, my anger would eventually go away. More importantly, in that hour's meeting, I'd truly realized not just that I was angry, but why. I was angry at Dennis and I was angry at Mr. Santini; I was angry at a lot of things. I was angry for the circumstances that had brought me to this point. With this realization about my anger, I just needed to figure out how to rid myself of it. The one defining moment in my discussion with the doctor had been that I was okay, and that I really didn't have any mental disease that could hamper me from achieving my dreams. I could not change my past, but I knew that I had control of the future in regards to the decisions that I made. My visit with that doctor had restored my faith and hope, in that I could learn from my mistakes and move forward with better judgment.

It was as though a large weight had been lifted from me that day, and I was a much lighter person as a result. I also looked around at the landscape and the bareness of the trees on that November day, and it was as though I was seeing everything for the first time. I had been bogged down with problems for so long that I'd forgotten about all of the beautiful things that life had to offer. Everything seemed so fresh and new as I inspected the bareness of the trees against the gray clouded sky, and the colorful leaves laying on the ground.

Later that day, my father called to make sure that I was alright. I am sure that the hospital had called him to let him know that I had attempted to sign myself in. I didn't tell him that I had been to the mental ward, but instead told him not to worry, and that everything was going to be alright. I didn't even tell Danielle about my visit to the hospital and my attempt to sign myself in, as I couldn't face the idea of disappointing one more person, and felt that this would best be kept sealed in my own memory vault.

Things changed for me after that difficult period in my life, and they started in a new direction. It was not easy, as nothing ever really is, but my attitude became more focused and I tried hard not to let things get me down. Just a few weeks after the visit to the mental ward, I received a call to interview for a job with an investment company that I had contacted during my job seeking attempts. Danielle helped to me to prepare for the interview and even drove me into city on that momentous day. We stopped at the mall on the drive into the city to get a makeover, and had lunch afterwards. I was thrilled to receive a call a week later, alerting me that I had gotten the job that I'd interviewed for and that I would start my new employment in January of 1986.

I'd finally gotten the break that I'd been looking for. I always look back at this period in my life as an important transitional stage in my development. Had I not met such two very different people that contrasted against one another so drastically, I may have stayed in my own version of purgatory for years. I really feel that I was fated to meet them, as they spurred me on in their own different ways and into a whole new direction in my life. Danielle was my moral compass in keeping me on track and helping me to navigate such a trying relationship with Dennis. Had I heeded her advice, I may not have been such a puppet in my relationship with Dennis. She also painted for me a picture as to what a true friend looked like, as I had never had such a close and intimate relationship with another woman – not like I'd had with her. She showed me the love and support that I needed to become confident in myself and my abilities, and through her guidance, I finally gained the confidence that I needed to become successful in reaching some of my goals.

Looking back at my relationship with Dennis, I better understand the importance of his place in my life. I learned the importance of self-respect in intimate relationships. Having the confidence to value yourself and your importance, so as not to be likened to a stop-and-go store. That confidence is far more attractive than a lack thereof, and will attract someone who you deserve to be with rather than someone who will treat you with disrespect. Through my interactions with Dennis, I also learned that you cannot make someone be the person who you want them to be. People usually don't change to suit your needs, regardless of your wishes.

With all of that in mind, it's hard to believe that it took me a few more years to wake up and smell the roses in regards to my relationship with Dennis. I found it difficult to break off my relationship with him, as I still had it in mind that we would be together someday. I was wanting something that he was not emotionally capable of delivering. I'd eventually learn that I also had a fear of commitment, as I was continually attaching myself to men who were not available – emotionally or physically. But, at the time, I continued an on-again and off-again relationship with him for the next three years, until I finally decided to move into Pittsburgh during one of our off-again moments.

I had made some friends at my new job and I saw a number of them in some good healthy relationships, and I'd also taken up racquetball to help get my anger out in a physical way, to the end that I was very aware of how I was treading through my life. After much evaluation and introspection, about myself and what I wanted in a relationship, I finally broke free from Dennis. I had missed some opportunities to go out with some nice men over this time, and had spent some valuable years hoping for something that never would be, but it finally came to me that the real "blessing in disguise" was that I had not ended up marrying Dennis.

May

My friendship with Danielle has been one of the longest lasting and consistent female relationships I have ever had. Danielle and Terri were so different in their outlooks on life, also, that they each offered me a new way of looking at things in regards to female bonding. The relationship with Terri ended with disappointment, but Terri's moments of caring remain etched into my mind. These two women were not replacements for the relationship that I had with my mother, but each acted as surrogates in times when I needed them the most. A lot of times, it was as though I had an older sister who was looking out for me, and so it was nice to have these relationships and to have someone to help advise me – I wish more than anything that I could have trusted them with my secrets. Had I done so, maybe things would have turned out differently for me.

Having Danielle and Terri in my life as soul sisters was fabulous; however, the relationship that I had with my sister was extra special. My bond with May was totally different in respect to my relationships with Danielle and Terri. May and I have been through a lot together, and share our family roots. Whenever I've needed support or stability, I've always been able to look to May. May went through some of the same trials and tribulations as I did, and outwardly she's generally seemed to handle her life without too many wrinkles. As her sister, I've known this isn't entirely true, as she for the most part has tended to hold everything inside.

I never thought much about how May handled things until later in life, but I did know that having May as my sister was one of the highlights of my life. In thinking about her and the bond that we

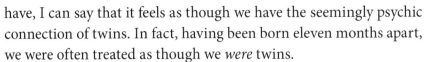

have, I can say that it feels as though we have the seemingly psychic connection of twins. In fact, having been born eleven months apart, we were often treated as though we *were* twins.

In speaking with May, it's often as though I'm listening to my own mind repeat something back to me, and it can feel as though she's the reflection of my own soul. We like the same things – from the way that we dress to the things that we like to eat – and it's often been said that we even have the same type of laugh. There are not too many things that we seem to have a real difference of opinion about, and I can't remember too many arguments that we had – if we did argue, fortunately, the disagreements didn't last too long. I don't ever want to make my sister truly angry with me, as I would miss having her in my life more than anything.

The fact is that growing up with May was fun. We laughed about everything and anything that could possibly be humorous. Sometimes our laughter was inappropriate, I admit, since, as kids, we would giggle in church at the untimeliest of moments. We would sometimes laugh uncontrollably about things that our mother said or did, or about the circumstances that we found ourselves in as a result of her behavior. Laughing was the way that May and I were able to cope with our mother's illness, though, and we would sometimes imitate or replay a situation in a dramatic fashion for each other's entertainment or that of our cousins. It was our way of relieving the stress of the situations in which we found ourselves.

Then, as adults, we found ourselves being the primary caregivers for our mother. Many times, after our father passed away, my sister and I had to arrive at a mental institution to find a very polished looking woman sitting amongst some very disheveled looking characters with some severe behavior disorders. And while we weren't making fun of the people in the unit, as we had lots of empathy for them and their situations, knowing firsthand what those families were going through, we would, however, laugh about the situation, as we were left to take care of things. It was strange how it could sometimes be the smallest thing that would provoke us into a fit of laughter.

Sometimes our mother would join in and get caught up in our

laughter also, depending on her mood or medication. Other times, during those visits our mother would look at both of us as though we'd done something terrible to her. We've both been the recipients, at one time or another, of a piercing stare – as though it was our fault that she was in the position that she was in. My mother would look at you as though her circumstances were all your fault, and as if you were the cause of her problems. I often wondered what she was thinking during those times. Privately, my sister and I would joke with each other about what we might have done to receive such a look from our mother.

I've always been thankful to have May in my life to navigate the situation with my mother, and I could not imagine having had to grow up in my household without having had May to share my childhood with. May is the one who kept things light, as I tended to be the more serious of the two of us. It seemed during our childhood that May's goal in life was to make me laugh, actually, and to make me laugh at the most inopportune of times. She was seemingly able to maintain her composure at all times, as I was the one that had a more difficult time controlling my emotions. When my father was alive, I would be the one who was scolded for any mischievous behavior that was prompted by May.

With me being the older of the two of us, it was made known to us by my father that I was the one who was to set the example for my little sister. Even though she was really not smaller in size than me, as we were both the same height. May and I were tall for our ages, and we both peaked at five foot eight in senior high. Her build was always a bit slimmer than mine, as I have a fuller build (like that of my mother), and my father always said that May was built like his mother and took after his side of the family. That statement would make me wonder if my father preferred May to me, but I always told myself that he loved us both the same.

May and I were both recognizable as we walked the halls of our high school since we each had a way of tilting our heads to the side that made us stand out. We were often chided by others in regards to the similarity. May followed me in school, as she was one grade behind me and, in many cases, had the same teacher that I would have had the year before. As a result, she sometimes felt that she had to live up to the expectations that I had set in the way of academics. I was an above average student and I was taking the academic program of study, as I was preparing to be a teacher. May became interested in business and was planning to obtain a job immediately after high school, so she finally landed in different classes when those separate plans came into effect. Nevertheless, everyone knew that we were sisters and that we participated in the same sports teams.

It was through my encouragement that she participated on the sports teams, though, and as a result she met a significant teacher and coach who would influence her life. When May became eligible, she joined the basketball and volleyball teams in which I participated. At that time, we started a friendly competition that was prompted by our coach, who was soon to become a prominent presence in both of our lives, even though I would say that he influenced the life of my sister more than he did mine.

I met Coach Fenton in my ninth-grade year at the tryouts for the senior high volleyball team. He taught myself and a group of my peers the basics of playing volleyball and some other pertinent moves to the games. After reviewing our skills and watching our attempts to perfect our skills, he chose his team members. I was at the bottom of the totem pole as far as class rank was concerned, but I was surprised to make the team and receive a starting position.

I believe that it was at this time that Coach Fenton influenced the career path of my sister. It was through his persuasion that she enrolled in almost all of his business classes the following semester. Coach Fenton was the head of the business department and he was always recruiting students for his classes. He had approached me about taking a few of his classes, as well; however, I wasn't interested in filling my schedule with courses that weren't pertinent to what I wanted to accomplish. I'm positive, though, that it was through his persuasion that my sister made a different decision than myself – not to follow the academic field of study, and to take business classes instead. I was a bit disappointed actually, as I'd hoped that she would join me at the college which I planned to attend. However, it was at this point that we started to go our different ways in our life journeys.

I think that my sister didn't feel at the time that she was college material, as her confidence in her grades fell just a little short in comparison to mine when it came to academics. Nevertheless, she excelled in her business classes, so it turned out well for her. And I imagine it was for the best – May always referred to me as a "bookworm" since she didn't really enjoy reading or studying as much as I did. She was more socially oriented at the time than I was.

Socially, I really paled in comparison to her, as May had a number of friends and, in her senior year, was nominated to be the president of her class. Her sense of humor made her easy to get along with, and other people were attracted to her easy-going manner. At that time, I was very shy and lacking in social confidence when it came to developing friendships with my classmates. May helped me to develop friendships with some of the friends that she had made outside of our sports teams, at least, and more often than not, I was included in the outings on which May was invited. Sometimes, I think that it may have been that they felt sorry for me and included me out of respect for my sister; I was well aware of my awkwardness in social situations, after all, and so I sometimes tried too hard to fit in with my peers. Most of the time, I would opt to just stay home rather than put myself in an uncomfortable situation.

On the other hand, my sister was not only popular with our teammates, but she also became a close friend of Coach Fenton's. I wasn't aware of this until Coach Fenton initiated an invite to our home for an evening meal, just prior to one of our home games. He'd hinted around to both my sister and I that he would love to come to our home for a home-cooked meal. I was a sophomore at the time and very hesitant for several reasons, regarding the idea of having him come to our home for dinner. I was worried as to how my mother would behave and I also wondered what Mr. Santini would think about the invite, as he hadn't received the same type of invitation. My sister, though, went ahead and made the invite to both Coach Fenton and to my history teacher at the time, who was the assistant coach. Interestingly, my father didn't seem to mind, as he'd already met both of our coaches and seemed to approve.

On the evening of the dinner, to my surprise, our mother stepped up to the occasion and prepared a lovely meal. She set out the good china in the formal dining room and everything looked beautiful. That particular day, she was in a good mood and was a gracious hostess to our guests. I still recall the relief that I felt, that nothing embarrassing took place in front of my teacher and coach. I sat on pins and needles the whole time, as I could hardly wait for the meal to be over so that we could make our exit to the evening game. I also remember a feeling of pride in regards to my mother, as she looked especially attractive that day and was particularly sociable with both men.

Both coaches were outgoing men, and they were very complimentary towards my mother – and of course she was flattered by the attention. She seemed to enjoy their visit and handled things well. My father didn't make it into the house on time for dinner, as it was earlier than his quitting time; I recall being nervous due to the lack of his presence, as he would have been able to smooth over anything of uncertainty that might have taken place. He arrived as we were getting ready to leave for the game, though, and he then showed up at the gymnasium later to cheer us on.

That dinner was in the fall of the year, and it was during the following summer that Coach Fenton started his visits to our home. May had started taking her classes with the coach in the spring, and she made the invitation. He had just gone through a divorce and, as a result, he became a regular dinner guest. Quite consistently, he would arrive in the afternoon to play golf or tennis and then land in the swimming pool with my sister and me. He would remain through dinner and then stay late, playing cards with my sister, my mother, and myself. A lot of times, I wouldn't be present, instead working at the dairy mart till eleven o'clock in the evening. My father didn't join us, regardless, as he remained in the living room watching television while everyone else was gathered around the kitchen table.

The situation was a bit strange, as my father didn't seem to interact much with Coach Fenton. I thought that maybe my father didn't mind, as my mother seemed to enjoy his company and she was on her best behavior for the most part. I don't remember too many times when she said or did anything too embarrassing in his presence. My sister shared with me recently that she had discussed our mother's illness with Coach Fenton and that she was the subject of many of their conversations. And even though May didn't share this with me at the time, I am happy that she had someone in whom to confide.

I had never discussed my mother's situation with Mr. Santini, as I never felt comfortable in having that conversation. I think that I was afraid what he might think. Early in my life, I was always very careful as to who I would share our family secret with. I think that my sister probably shared it with Coach Fenton because he had such a presence in our home at that time. She may have wanted him to be aware of our mother's illness in case anything unusual took place.

Coach Fenton just seemed to slide right into our home, though, as his relationship with my sister and myself seemed acceptable to both of our parents. Early in his visits to our home, I was included in the outdoor activities – until one summer day came and my sister became annoyed that I was going to join them for a game of golf. She made it known to me that she wanted to play with the coach alone. I insisted on going along anyway, and ended up being made to feel like the third wheel by my sister. Coach Fenton didn't seem to mind my presence and interacted with me just the same as always. It was at that time that I became aware that there was something more to their relationship than what my sister had wanted me to know about. Having my own relationship with Mr. Santini, though, I respected those boundaries and made myself scarce from then on out.

To what extent their relationship evolved, I wasn't exactly sure. May never shared with me any of the details about their outings, so it was just left to my imagination. Once I felt like an intruder, I also became a bit irritated with my parents. I didn't understand why my father didn't mind that Coach Fenton was permitted to play golf on such a regular basis while Mr. Santini was treated with such caution. I

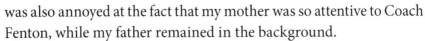

was also annoyed at the fact that my mother was so attentive to Coach Fenton, while my father remained in the background.

Coach Fenton also made little comments to me about my sudden lack of interest in playing golf and tennis with them, and my mother made allegations on several occasions that Coach Fenton was interested in me. I emphatically denied that he had any interest in me at all, arguing that it was May who he was interested in. I was humiliated that she would think such a thought and make such a comment to her teenage daughter; her comments infuriated me, really, and caused me to start to have some dislike for Coach Fenton. I couldn't believe how he'd managed to charm his way into our home, and I wasn't sure of his intentions toward my sister. I felt some need to protect her from him, but I wasn't exactly sure of what I was protecting her from.

Coach Fenton was aware of my friendship with Mr. Santini and privately, from time to time, made little comments about the attention that he paid me. He had noticed the interactions that we had in the gym during the season, and knew of our familiarity with each other. I didn't give him the satisfaction of a reaction to his comments, as I wasn't about to reveal my true feelings. Thus, I ignored his remarks that, at times, were very demeaning of Mr. Santini. Just from the interactions that I had witnessed between the two of them at school, I knew that they were not very fond of each other, even if I wasn't exactly sure of the reason behind it. I often wondered if Coach Fenton had spoken to my parents in regards to my relationship with Mr. Santini, as he certainly had ample opportunity. The point that I am trying to make is that my sister and I were treated very differently in regards to our relationships with our teachers and coach, and I found it all very difficult to grasp when it came to the acceptance of a man who I was beginning to despise.

I truly wasn't sure if anything was taking place between Coach Fenton and my sister, though, and I wondered what my parents thought. To my knowledge, they never made any mention of his interest in her. He spent two summers with us, though, the situation continuing until things changed when my sister suddenly took an interest in one of the neighbor boys. In her junior year, she was invited to the homecoming by Tom, who lived three miles down the road. They had become friendly at school and it seemed to me that the friendship with the coach was fading into the background as a result. He was no longer coming to our home on such a regular basis. The coach's final visit was to deliver a beautiful oil painting of a windmill that existed on the club property. That visit seemed to signify the end of things as they'd been between my sister and the coach.

It was only a few weeks after the delivery of that gift that I learned the news from my sister that Coach Fenton was getting married. I was stunned by the news, and even more surprised as to who he was marrying. May shared that he had impregnated a senior high student from the other end of the school district; the student was the same age as my sister was at the time, and the timing of the announcement was confusing to me. He had spent so much time at our home with my sister, I wondered how he'd managed to get the other girl pregnant at all. How my sister learned of this information, I wasn't exactly sure; she seemed to be just as surprised as I was about the engagement. Her surprise made me wonder about their relationship and if the Coach's blemished reputation had been the cause of their parting. Either way, Coach Fenton certainly had some mystery surrounding his romantic interludes. During the previous school year, there had also been some gossip about him dating a fellow teacher in our building. I wondered if that news in itself had caused my sister to seek out another male friend.

Really, though, I wondered what his attraction was for the women who he was involved with. In my eyes, he wasn't the perfect specimen of physical attraction. I surmised that the attraction must have been found in the way that he charmed women with his words. The image that I still carry in my mind is of him in his gray sweatsuit that bagged in the rear end and his sweatshirt that hugged his broad shoulders. He was always hiking up his sweatpants, as they didn't seem to fit properly, and he was a bit on the portly side, his frizzy hair always looking like it needed a good coat of conditioner. And he had a mustache that he liked to twist while deep in thought. I could see where someone could be attracted to his personality, though, as he liked to joke around, making sarcastic remarks that you either liked or you didn't. Still, I would question why a grown man would want to hang around with teenage girls on such a frequent basis. That being said, of course, I never actually witnessed anything taking place that would have been deemed inappropriate... but it was just the weirdness of it all. The amount of time that they spent together made me question the type of relationship that they had.

Then, there wasn't as much secrecy involved as there was between myself and Mr. Santini. In observing Coach Fenton, I could see the attraction that he held for May on his face, and I knew that he really did care about her. But, I often wondered if he talked with her in the same way that Mr. Santini talked with me about his desires. It also crossed my mind, at times, if he ever acted on the affection that he held for her, and if so, to what lengths. My thought now is that it might have just been playful fanfare, as it ended so suddenly, and the lasting emotional effects seemed to be nonexistent when compared to those of the long involvement I had with Mr. Santini.

I'm sharing all of this with you because I'm happy that my sister was able to move on quickly from her friendship with Coach Fenton and on into a relationship that would become permanent for her. May was very different from me, as she was able to let things go; she didn't let her relationship with Coach Fenton tarnish her ability to move on with her life. I really do not know what the depth of their friendship was, but she didn't seem too bothered that he ended his time with us. There was no lingering either, as she was fully engaged in the relationship that she had with Tom. Her courtship with him seemed relatively normal, and it blossomed over time.

When May started dating Tom, though, my relationship with May changed slightly since she was spending more time with him and away from our home. Once I departed to go to college, their relationship became even tighter. May also bonded with Tom's family, and they were very demanding of the time that she spent with them. She quickly became entrenched in their family traditions and was the daughter that Tom's mother had craved, as she had five sons and no daughters.

Upon her graduation from high school, May got her first job at a bank and was quite successful in her new position. Tom was a year behind May in high school but, upon graduation in 1979, he proposed to my sister. He had received a scholarship to play football for a local college, and after their marriage they would be moving. Tom was working for my father during the summer months to make some extra money, and they lived with my parents due to the size of our large house, whereas his parents had a smaller home and they couldn't accommodate them. My visits would be few and far between, but I would try to catch them on my rare visits home from college.

We wouldn't reunite under the same roof until the spring of 1981. May became pregnant and was excited to be expecting her first child. She was preparing for the birth, due in February of 1981, and she came back to live with my parents since the hospital in which she planned to give birth was close by. I had graduated from college and was back in the family home, as well. Our lives had taken such different turns, as I was starting my career and she was starting a family. I was very happy for her, though, and also anxious to meet my new nephew.

May and I were so much alike in so many different ways that I never expected our lives to be so different. May was able to stabilize her life with a marriage and the start of a family. It was that summer that I headed for the Jersey Shore, only to fill my life with more confusion. I left that summer, as I was feeling so alone even though I was surrounded my people who loved me. That love was hard to recognize, I now realize, as my mother was having some issues related to her condition, Martin and Terri were getting a divorce, and my sister and her husband had moved in with the new baby. I was not sure of my future, and everything seemed to be a bit much. Feeling as though I needed to find myself, I took off for an adventure with no thought of the consequences. Thinking back on that time, I can't believe that I just packed my car and left without any clear direction or job to support me. It's no wonder that my father was concerned about my well-being, and probably confused as to why I was leaving.

I often wonder why I felt the need to escape that small town in search of something different. I didn't know why I couldn't just be like my sister May and be happy with marrying a local boy and settling into a family life. The friendships that we had with our respective teachers influenced us in such different ways, though. Mr. Santini's announcement of the new addition to his family with his wife didn't stop the fascination between us. However, with the announcement of Coach Fenton's marriage and pregnancy, the course of my sister's life seemed to change entirely.

I wish that I would have been able to cut the ties so quickly as she did, and move on with my life. To this day, I really don't know to what extent my sister was involved with that coach and if it ever turned sexual or romantic. On the other hand, I also never really shared all the details of the involvement that I had with Mr. Santini. Regardless, we are still very much alike in spite of the different paths that we have taken.

In retrospect, what went on with my sister and myself and these two teachers would not be acceptable behavior in today's society. My mother was not in her right mind and then found all of the attention to be flattering. She may have even thought that Coach Fenton was interested in her. My father, I am sure, didn't know what to think about the interest that these men were paying to his daughters and wife, but it was also a different time. My father probably didn't know how to handle the situation, and didn't want to cause any problems. And of course, my parents may have received a warning about Mr. Santini and his interest towards me, but on the contrary, Coach Fenton presented himself as a respectable man – and he was single, so it may have made things alright in their minds. In the small town in which I grew up, girls married young and raised families at an early age, as we were in farm country. Maybe that's what made it all seem so normal.

In knowing May, I can say that she also seemed to make my childhood seem normal. Growing up with her as my sister, I could always count on her as we navigated our childhood together. With us having dealt with some of the same situations, there is a bond between us that no one else would understand, and we have remained close to each other even though we now live hundreds of miles apart. Connecting regularly on the phone and through visits that are too few and far apart, we still always seem to know when the other one is suffering in some way or experiencing great joy. Sometimes, the connection is so strong that we arrive to visit each other in the same top or shoes that we bought separately and without the other one knowing. I don't ever expect our thought waves about each other to disappear, and I would be saddened if they did.

We still have the same close bonds that we had in our childhood, sometimes much to the envy of our respective spouses since they occasionally feel left out when we are together. Laughter is still a big part of our healing together too, as we still laugh at the same things that sometimes no one else understands outside of the two of us. And we both wish that we didn't live so far apart, as we provide healing for each other from the wounds of our past that nobody else can offer.

William

May and I were so similar in nature that it sometimes made me think about our family dynamics. I never really questioned why May and I were able to remain close, but I did reminisce about my brother, William. I wondered if the wounds from our past had harbored the inconsistencies in our relationship. My relationship with William over the years had at times been distant, and I thought maybe it had something to do with the incident in the chicken coop. In pondering our childhood, I wondered if maybe my mother held him responsible for that incident, and I thought about how it had affected his relationships – not only with me, but with the other women in his life.

In thinking back, I realized that it was only after my brother Martin left for the army that William was left to contend with myself and my sister. My mother shared with me at different times throughout my life that there was some jealousy on the part of my brother. She told me that he felt left out, as May and I received a lot of the attention. I was too young to know what might have transpired between my mother and my brother in regards to that jealously, but I am sure that he felt like an outsider, as May and I would always stick together when William attempted to test us during our childhood years. May and I were so close in age as compared to the seven-year age difference between William and I. He probably felt, at times, like he was being double-teamed as a result.

Interestingly, as William and I were the two middle children, we see-sawed back and forth between fighting and getting along together. We could have some really nasty battles with each other, as

I could be quite a tomboy and I wasn't about to let anyone bully me. Our fights could be fairly rough, as we would hit and punch each other. Of course, I was the one on the losing end since I wasn't as strong as him and couldn't compete with his physical build.

One particular incident that's still clear in my mind happened when I was about eight years old. One summer afternoon, William and I took to teasing each other and it quickly progressed to chasing each other with buckets of water. I drenched him with some water and then darted up onto the back porch to escape retribution. He caught up with me and pushed me over the top of the porch railing, which offered something of a six foot drop to the ground. On my way to the hard ground below, I scraped my rib cage on the edge of the wooden porch floor and as a result scraped my entire left rib cage. My ribs received quite a bruise and the skin covering my ribs got pretty brush-burned. My ribs hurt for several weeks afterward, and the skin took quite a while to heal.

The most hurtful bruise was to my feelings, though, as William never apologized to me; nor did he even check to see if I had been hurt. After pushing me over the banister railing, he just disappeared. The next day when I went to the club swimming pool in my two-piece bathing suit, by brother's girl crush took notice of my wound. I of course reenacted the previous day's event with her and expressed displeasure regarding the actions of my brother. William learned a few days later that I'd shared the incident with her, as she was no longer interested in his attention. Secretly, I found a little pleasure in destroying his chances with his love interest, given that I was still angry with him for not apologizing to me.

William had impeccable timing in knowing when he could get away with fighting with me, as my parents never seemed to be around when these encounters took place. The only evidence that something had happened was if I ended up in tears or received the physical evidence of bruises that could be left behind. It's normal to have some fights with your siblings, obviously, but the ones I had with William could escalate quickly. May and I could have a few physical episodes, but we would always end up laughing until one of us would relent.

William simply didn't relent, and our fights would last until I was in tears. May didn't have such problems with William and, being the older sister, I usually interceded on her behalf anyway. May was smarter than myself in that respect, and knew that there was no winning in this type of warfare. I came to realize that my brother had problems in learning to control his moods, though, and I somehow agitated him.

May was somehow not as sensitive to the teasing, and would just let things roll off of her shoulders. In comparison, I took everything to heart and felt that I needed to defend every comment that William made toward me. I couldn't just let it go – I had to take the bait of any teasing that would take place until it would escalate to being out of control. As I matured, I tried not to get into verbal battles with William because I'd learned that they would always lead to a physical confrontation. I don't ever recall him being the great protector as an older brother either; once he got into high school, he really didn't want much to do with his younger sisters. We were more of a nuisance for him than anything.

I recall one particular incident which highlights how we could be his irritants. I was in the fifth grade at the time, and my brother had just started dating. He had brought a girlfriend to the house one evening to visit, and it was around the Christmas holiday; my sister and I had received wigs for Christmas. The wigs that we'd received had come packaged with Styrofoam head forms that the long blond wigs rested on when not in use. This particular afternoon, we got the bright idea to put a hanger through the bottom of the Styrofoam and to attire them with robes so they would each have a body. We took the outfitted dummies upstairs, to the floor above where my brother was sitting with his newest of girlfriends. We then dangled the dummies from the window to the bottom floor, where they could view our creations. The first time, they found it to be funny, but we progressed on to parading the dummies around the room in which they were sitting and basically making nuisances out of ourselves. It got to the point that William got so irritated with us that he took his girlfriend and left the house. Thinking back on it, I realize May and I could at times really get on his nerves.

William not only struggled with his moods, but also with his academic studies; however, he found his talent to be in auto mechanics and excelled in the trade school that he attended. Early in his junior high years, failing attempts at getting good grades caused some dissention in our household between William and my father, though I'm not entirely sure if it was his grades or his mischievous behavior that caused my father to dish out some punishment. Compared to the trouble that teenagers get themselves into today, though, there's no comparison. Nevertheless, at that time, it was pretty common to get a few smacks for misbehaving. I am sure that he may have felt singled out, too, as Martin hadn't received such punishment as often as William did. In comparison to his siblings, I bet he often felt that he was being treated unfairly.

For whatever reason, I know William always felt like he was the black sheep of the family, and this affected our relationship. Over the years, William has had strained relations with all of his siblings, as well as both of our parents at one time or another. When my father was alive, he worked hard to make sure that he treated all of his children with the same type of love and care, and he went out of his way to understand my brother and make sure he felt like he was part of the family unit. Yet, I also know that my father found him just as hard to understand at various times, even as he continued to work on his relationship with him until his final days. But, there was always separation between William and the rest of the family.

During my high school years, William was not a strong presence in my life, as he had moved out of our family home upon his graduation from high school. He immediately took a job at a local garage, working on cars. It wasn't too long after that when he married his high school sweetheart and settled into married life. His wife was very sweet, and extremely quiet and shy. I found it hard to get to know her, as I was shy around her and our interactions were very limited. She was a pretty girl, though, with light, long blond hair and freckles which were in contrast to the dark-haired William. My brother had grown into a handsome man, as he had rich dark brown hair and brown eyes with strong facial features. At that time, he had an athletic build and a witty sense of humor which shined when he was in the right frame of mind. I share this with you now, as they seemed like an odd pairing right from the start. She seemed so reserved when paired against my brother's more outgoing personality.

This was the first marriage of five marriages that my brother would have. I won't bore you with all of the details in regards to all of his marriages, as they're fairly similar in how they appeared to our family. They would typically start out well and then end suddenly, and without any clear warning. Up until the point of a marriage failing, he'd participated sporadically in family get-togethers such as picnics, holidays, etc. After his marriage would dissolve, we wouldn't see him for a long period of time. His first marriage lasted seven years, and ended one day after their home was damaged by a strong flood of rapid water. The flood not only damaged their home, but destroyed their marriage, as well. I recollect that William made a sudden disappearance on the day of the flood, and left his wife stranded to deal with everything. Afterwards, my father tried hard to intercede in helping to repair both their marriage and their home, but my brother didn't want anything to do with anyone. I don't know what caused my brother to leave and, as I recall, his wife was distraught at her sudden turn of circumstances. She was left to pick up the pieces in regards to their home and the aftermath of their marriage, and I felt sorry for her, as it took a long time for her to recover from the way my brother had treated her. Our relatives didn't understand my brother either, or his strange way of dealing with things.

It was during William's second marriage that I had the most interaction with him and his wife. I was in my second year of college when he married Betsy. Betsy was a successful business woman and was divorced with two teenagers that were getting ready to start college themselves. Betsy was tall, attractive and outgoing, and a bit older than William. Her personality was quite different from his previous wife's and she had a warm, mothering type of personality. I immediately liked her, as she was easy to get to know and she also took a liking to me, as well. I thought that William might have been attracted to her because of those coddling traits she exhibited that I thought he could have missed in his childhood years. Betsy included me in some of their outings and made every effort for them to be involved in family get-togethers; she came to our home and included her father, and we went to their home to visit on a regular basis. It was nice to share those bonds with her family.

Betsy was always trying to be helpful to me, and she came to New Jersey with her daughter during that summer when I went to the seashore. She saw my living conditions with the other girls and encouraged me to gather my belongings and come back home, though I wasn't ready to go home at the time and didn't heed her advice. I don't know whether it was my father who sent her to try and retrieve me or if it was Betsy's idea, as it was a surprise. I enjoyed their visit, though, and felt that she really cared about my well-being, given that she'd gone to the trouble of making that eight hour trip to see me. Normally, I would have caved in and taken the advice, but I was simply in a different state of mind and wanted to continue my adventure.

At one point, I was able to help Betsy and William out of a financial jam in regards to a car that my brother had purchased. In the summer prior to my senior year of college, William approached me with a deal in regards to a brand-new car that he had purchased a few months earlier. He told me that I could use it for my senior year of college, as I needed a car for my student teaching, the only requirement being that I took over the payments when I got out of school. Without too much thought, I agreed, as the car was beautiful and a dream come true. I hadn't been sure what I was going to do in regards to the transportation required to get back and forth for student teaching, and so the timing was perfect. I really didn't give much thought to the cost of the car and the insurance that I would have to carry, and didn't receive much advice in that regard either. Thankfully, at the end of graduation, I was able to get a job – as my brother had presented me with the payment books, which were in his name. Fortunately, I was still living at home at the time and I was able to make the payments. In hindsight, I should have given the deal more consideration, as a good portion of my paycheck went to making those car payments. I also helped to build up my brother's credit and not my own.

My brother had purchased and now owned his own gas station and garage where he was the chief mechanic. I made every effort to take my car to his garage, and I sometimes took a precious day off and drove quite a distance in order to have only him service my car. He would charge me for the service and treat me at times like I was a pain in the rear, as he would barely say two words to me. I would often leave his service station feeling like I was a bother, depending on his mood. He was my brother, though, and I was trying to help him out as much as I could, even if I sometimes asked myself why I was going so far out of my way to accommodate someone who seemed not to care. I wasn't aware at the time of the financial difficulties that he was having with his business; he was going through some rough times, as we learned from Betsy. It was not long after my arrival back from New Jersey that Betsy invited my parents and my siblings to their home. William wasn't present at the time, but she had prepared a nice meal to accompany the announcement of their divorce. Betsy shared with us that William had difficulties with managing money and that their differences of opinion in regards to money were just too great for them to overcome. She said that she loved William, but that she wanted to retire in the future and that he wasn't able to have any self-control in regards to spending money. We were sorry to learn of their divorce, and I was sorry that Betsy would no longer be part of my life.

I only learned recently that William wasn't aware of this dinner that Betsy gave in order for her family to share the news with us. Once again, we'd just thought that William had made himself scarce, as we never really knew if he would show up for a family event. With the divorce, he disappeared again; more often than not, it would be months before we would hear from him or see him again. My father would always hunt him down and somehow learn of his whereabouts.

William would just reappear when he had another woman who he wanted us to meet.

William could also get upset with us if we changed the family get-togethers to a home other than that of our mother. My sister or Terri would sometimes host a holiday in their own home, and William would simply be irritated that it wasn't being held in the family home. Any such change of plans would set him off and he'd pout during the entire dinner, not even bother to show up, or else leave after feeling put out for some reason. Because of his inconsistencies in mood and behavior, my sister and I began to suspect that he had some condition similar to that of our mother, even if we weren't exactly sure what the diagnosis would be – but his pattern of behavior deemed some medical name, in our opinions.

Despite his casting us aside, though, we attended all of his weddings that we were invited to and welcomed each wife into our lives. I didn't become close to the last few of his wives, however, as I'd by that point gotten married myself and so we lived quite a distance apart. William was invited to my wedding, but he wrote me a letter telling me that he couldn't attend because of family issues. I wasn't exactly sure what he was referring to, but accepted his vague reasoning.

Another separation from family came in the fact that William didn't like my sister's husband, as he was mechanically inclined and would help my father with his vehicle from time to time. William would make promises to take care of something and then not follow through in a timely fashion, and so Tom would step in and handle the situation, but it caused some friction. One Christmas Day, William left our holiday dinner because he felt steamed as a result of learning that Tom had worked on my father's car. We didn't know his feelings at the time, though, and William didn't enlighten us; rather, his sudden departure left us all wondering what had set him off this time. Holidays could be interesting times, as not only could my mother be in a mood, but my brother could make things interesting with his own antics.

My brother William didn't like my brother-in-law Tom for other reasons, as well. Tom worked for my father for many years after he graduated from college. He'd been offered a teaching position but turned it down, as he wanted to manage the club when my father retired. In 1995, my father retired earlier than he had planned as a result of Tom telling the club board members that my father wasn't fit to do his job anymore. As you can imagine, this caused quite a bit of tension between Tom and my father, as well as with my sister. My sister stood by her husband, though, and thus a family rift was created. My brothers weren't very fond of Tom for his betrayal of my father, but somehow my living at a distance kept me out of all of the family drama and I didn't have to get involved in choosing sides. I simply loved my father and supported him from afar.

My father, being the honorable man that he was, retired as a result of Tom's complaint. They had a very lovely party at the club for him and it was a memorable night, as he received the accolades that he deserved for all of his years of service. Prior to that important evening, he'd also mended his strained relationship with May and Tom. Everyone attended that momentous dinner except for William, and I was disappointed on my father's behalf that William didn't care enough to attend such an important dinner in recognition of my father.

As funny as it may seem, I have been the only one through the years that has remained in somewhat consistent contact with William. For many years, I was very similar to my father in trying to keep our family together. I have always pursued my brother and have kept in touch in an attempt to not make him feel like the black sheep, but at times it has been a struggle to even have conversation, as he sometimes doesn't respond with too much interest in what I have to say. I often ask myself why I care and why I bother to attempt including him in my life, but he's also surprised me on several occasions in wanting to visit with me and my husband. I've always welcomed him and any of his significant others into my home. I love my brother unconditionally and have accepted him for who he is; I cannot change how other people behave and can only treat them the way that I would like to be treated, so I try hard to keep the lines of communication open and to let him know that he is loved.

As for communication regarding what happened in that chicken coop, I will probably never have that discussion with him. I don't hold him responsible for that incident, it was so long ago, and I have never dwelled on it. It didn't affect any of my relationships on a physical level, so far as I know, as one might think it could have. It happened so long ago and I was so young that I feel that my family simply swept it under the carpet. I think that they thought I was so young that I might not even remember what had happened to me. As for my brother, he was in those formative years of puberty, and his memory is, I'm sure, more vivid. Maybe there were words between my mother and my brother as a result and he was made to feel responsible, but in those days, things that happened in your family were just not discussed openly – as with my mother's illness. Things just got swept under the carpet instead, and I am sure it may have been the same with this situation.

I often think that William may have been ashamed of himself for not being the protector and saving me from harm. That is what big brothers are supposed to do, after all. Nevertheless, I walked on eggshells with my mother while growing up and I'm pretty sure that's what I'm doing with my brother. I'm happy to do it, though, as I don't want to bring anything up that would cause us to have a separation in response only to something that happened a long time ago. In my heart, I hope that my brother has been able to let the past go, as I don't blame him and I don't have any hard feelings as a result.

Currently, I live quite a distance from my brother and I don't see him very often. William and his wife of five years came to visit me this past year, but I hadn't met her previously even though she'd been a consistent presence in my brother's life. During their visit, I found out that she was the one who my brother always turned to for support in those down times during his life and in between all of his other marriages. She loves him unconditionally, with all of his scars, blemishes, and wounds. His wife was also instrumental in encouraging him to visit our mother after eighteen years of separation. My mother is ninety-two years old now, and I am so happy that they have been able to make amends.

As for our relationship... during his recent visit, we were able to have several conversations about our perspectives on growing up in our household, and finally able to talk about how each of us felt. We also discussed his various marriages and I got to understand both sides of the story, as he'd never shared his portion. I'm still not sure what I believe in regards to my brother and his relationships with women, but at least I've now heard his side of the story in regards to his marriages, as the endings had always been mysterious and seemed to be pointing fingers his way. As to the definitive cause of the break-ups – that will probably remain under debate.

Nevertheless, my brother feels that we are close, as we have always been in touch; and, I love him, and our phone calls have recently become more consistent. I hope and pray that he will reconcile with my siblings, as well, as life is too short to hold a grudge. I know my brother, like myself, has had many scrapes, bruises, and blemishes, and I'm glad that he has not let them break him. He has managed to stay in the light and not let the darkness completely overtake him, and for this I am proud of him.

My Love Story

Knowing what you know about my relationships with the men in my life, you may wonder what kind of a man I chose to marry. You may even wonder why I would even think of getting married! I know I sometimes swore I was never getting married as a result of a bad breakup; the men who I had met and surrounded myself with at various times were very different than the type of man that I wanted to marry, after all. I also knew that I had been emotionally damaged by some of the relationships that I had endured over the years.

In my eyes, my father was such a saint that I'd always known it would be hard for someone else to measure up to those standards. But, while it took a long time, I finally realized that I had a big fear of commitment, and had made choices in men that reflected that fear. In retrospect, much of my direction may have originated from my dealings with Mr. Santini, leading to other relationships that were lacking in real value. It took a fair amount of time for me to get out of this cycle. After my relationship with Dennis in 1984, I dated a variety of men for the next ten years. Those ten years were filled with some difficult relationships and struggles, but none like what I'd experienced with Dennis. My experiences with men were always intense and interesting to say the least, and they generally left me with some new insight in regards to relationships, at least. Yet, it wasn't until I started dating my husband at the age of thirty-six, in 1994, that my life became more balanced and I finally felt secure.

In spite of the different types of marriages I'd witness and the men who I'd encountered up until this point, I still had the fantasy of marrying a wonderful man. I'd had so many negative experiences with men that I don't know how else it could have happened, though. Meeting my husband Alex was the biggest manifestation of a miracle that has ever happened to me.

In June of 1994, exactly one month prior to the events leading up to the most romantic timeframe of my life, I invited my parents for a very special dinner, as I had an important announcement to make. At that dinner, in the most serious of tones, I shared with my parents that I was never getting married and that I was never having children. I told them that I'd had enough of disappointments in regards to men, and that meeting a great man was just not in the cards for me. They were so sweet to sit and listen as I shared my trials and tribulations in regards to my most recent dating disasters! I shared with them that I'd had enough heartbreaks and that I was just not meant to have that type of special relationship in my life; I also apologized to them for any expectations that they may have held for me on the subject. They already had two grandsons, and I shared that they would not be getting anymore. Both of my parents seemed to understand where I was coming from, as they looked at me with sympathy in their eyes. I know that they wanted me to meet someone to share my life with, but more than anything, they wanted me to be happy.

Ironically, it was not even a month later when I started to date my soon to be husband. As unbelievable as it all seemed to me at the time, it was someone who I had known for a long time. Strangely, it was through my work environment that I encountered Alex. I had spent the last ten years of my life working at the same investment firm that had given me my first break. I had remained in the same department that I'd started in and, as a result, gotten nice salary increases and bonuses along the way – with lots of recognition as a sales leader. Up until meeting Alex, I had guarded myself against getting involved with anyone who I worked with because of previous experiences.

He surprised me, though. I'd spoken to Alex over the telephone for the last few years on a near daily basis, giving him the daily rates and sales figures for his sales territory. Alex was a vice-president who managed the Eastern sales territory, and he was based in Columbus and worked out of his home office as a manager for his sales team. I knew who he was and had seen him at some of the formal functions that I'd attended, but we had never had a proper introduction until I was invited to attend a business function in New York that was being hosted by one of Alex's sales representatives. I remember being excited about the invitation and the opportunity to get to truly meet Alex.

Over the telephone, we arranged to have our plane seats together on our flight out of the local airport. Upon our first meeting, I was immediately impressed with what a handsome and distinguished looking gentleman he was. He was impeccably dressed in a very nice fitting suit with shoes that were shined to the point that you could see your own reflection. His eyes smiled with warmth and personality upon our meeting, and I immediately felt a connection with him, as well as very comfortable in his presence – simply, he was very endearing. We chatted on the plane about the basic things that one would talk about when getting to know someone. It was very easy to talk with him and I felt like I had known him forever.

Upon our arrival in New York, the event that we were attending got rained out and delayed until the following day. We spent the evening in rooms right beside each other in the hotel. The following day was still a rainy one and we were confined to the hotel, but I met him for breakfast and we talked for most of the day and got to know each other even more. Alex had been married before and he shared photos of his children with me, as he was very proud of them.

The event was cancelled and re-planned for the following week. On the plane ride home, I remember thinking to myself that I wished that I could meet someone like Alex. He was sixteen years older than me and was currently involved with a woman who he was planning to marry, and I was dating someone on a sporadic basis, though it wasn't really working out – as I was about to discover that he was already living with a flight attendant.

The following week, Alex and I set out once again to attend the event that had previously been cancelled. We arranged to sit with each other on the plane once again and it was as though we were already old friends. The following day, I played tennis with a group while Alex went sailing with another group of clients. That evening, though, we attended a dinner with everyone and I remember how sweet he was in placing his sport coat around my shoulders as we got out into the cool evening air, it being the fall of the year. I had such an enjoyable and remarkable time in getting to know Alex on a personal level. At the end of the two-day event, we parted at the airport to return to our regular roles and I felt a sense of sadness in knowing I wouldn't see him again, at least in the immediate future.

I didn't know it at the time, but things were about to dramatically change for me. After having the opportunity to be out in the field and discovering a new dimension to work, I applied for an outside sales position. It was a great opportunity to advance my career, but the downside was that I would be placed in some strange city in the United States. I had a good chance of getting a positon based on my experience and success with the company, though. The determination of the territory that you would be sent to was not revealed until you completed your additional training, but rumor had it that I was going to receive a position... and I was being considered for the Chicago territory.

The interview process was quite extensive, and it was taking a great deal of time for the final steps to be completed. I was very nervous and excited about the opportunity, but at the same time I wasn't really wanting to move so far away from my family. To make matters more complicated, a big surprise was about to be announced in my present position. My current sales director announced that she was leaving and that a new sales director was coming in from an outside territory. It was only a few days later that Alex was introduced as the new sales vice president for our department. I was floored by the news that he was going to be our new director, and I couldn't believe the timing of the announcement. It all happened just as I was moving ahead with my plans to leave the department and start a new adventure.

It didn't take long for him to settle into his new role and I felt obligated to share the news that I would be taking an outside role. He wasn't pleased with the decision, as I had been a star in the department and he wasn't interested in losing me, given that I would have been helpful in his adjustment. He ultimately asked me to stay in the department and promised me the opportunity to become a s sales manager. I was put in an uncomfortable position, as my deal for the outside positon was almost signed and sealed, but it was time for me to make an important decision in regards to the future of my career. The truth was that I was a little nervous about relocating to an unknown city and being so far away from my family, and the company could have me transferred anywhere in the United States – and there was no guarantee that I'd ultimately be happy with the decision. I thought long and hard about the opportunity that Alex was presenting to me as a potential manager, and then I decided to stay.

I do have to say that my decision was not received well by the CEO of the company, as their plans were being solidified for the outside team and I'd just thrown a monkey wrench into their plans. Thus, after turning down the outside sales position, I was now bound to excelling even more in my current position, as I had to prove to Alex that I was management material. Alex made sure that I got sent out of the office on some other outside sales trips in order to keep me happy and interested in my role, though, as he knew that I loved to travel and was able to arrange such opportunities as he saw fit.

As Alex settled into his new position, I was helpful in sharing as much information about our department as I possibly could. It was through these interactions that we became more familiar with each other and our personal situations in regards to dating. He was living with a woman and they were engaged to be married in the near future, and I was dating several different men. Yet, I noted an air of jealousy from Alex one day when I received a dozen roses from a man who I was seeing. At the same time, Alex had brought his fiancé into the office one day prior to an office get-together and I'd made her acquaintance, so we were well aware of one another's attachments.

As time went on, though, after work happy hours became a regular part of our work week, and Alex would join myself and a few other co-workers on a regular basis. One snowy day, he offered to drive me home, as I'd shared that I needed to catch my bus. I was hesitant at first, but he insisted and I was happy for the ride home. He dropped me in front of the carriage home in which I was living at the time and I made no offer to invite him inside. When I got inside of my home, however, I thought about him for a moment – and I realized that I had some sort of feelings for him, though I washed them out of my mind, as he was my boss. I didn't want any complications in that regard, as it reminded me of the time I'd had in the school district with the principal. I certainly didn't want history to repeat itself.

Little did I realize that things in my part of the world were about to get very complicated. After I received the roses at work from a professional football player, I could feel some annoyance on the part of Alex based on a few jabs he made about who I was seeing. I don't know what his problem was in that regard, but he suddenly wanted to introduce me to one of his best friends as a potential date. Alex's friend Jerry was newly divorced and Alex wanted me to go out on a double-date with him and his fiancé Ann. I had met Ann briefly and she had given me the once-over as though she was sizing up her competition; for her part, Ann was short, shapely, and attractive with stylish bobbed hair. She was about a decade younger than Alex with an outgoing, feisty personality based on what I'd initially perceived.

I was hesitant to meet Jerry, though, as I didn't want any complications in regards to my job or with my boss. Nevertheless, with the persuasion of Alex, I agreed to go to dinner on a double-date. Jerry lived in Ohio and was coming into town for the weekend, and so the date was all set. Alex arranged for me to meet them at his home, and we would go to dinner from there. The day of the date, I was a bit nervous about the whole ordeal and I kept kicking myself for getting myself into such a predicament. However, I went ahead with the plan and arrived at Alex's home to meet Jerry, and also to get better acquainted with Ann.

Alex had a beautiful contemporary home situated in the suburbs of the city and at the very height of the development in which he lived. The inside of his home was nicely decorated and very neat and orderly, just as I imagined. It wasn't your traditionally styled home and I loved the uniqueness of the layout. Meeting Jerry was an interesting experience, as he had a bold way about him and I didn't know how to deal with his sense of humor. I could immediately sense that he was all about humor and I didn't quite know how to joust back with him. I will say that I wasn't physically attracted to him, as he wasn't my type and I don't think that I was his either. I felt a bit awkward and, to make matters worse, Ann was still sizing me up. When Alex and Jerry left the room to gather their belongings to go to dinner, Ann made a strange comment. She looked me squarely in the face and said, "Did Alex tell you that I locked him in the basement?"

It was an interesting question that sent questions spiraling through my mind. Such as, why would you lock someone in the basement and was it on purpose? I don't even think that I acknowledged what I heard, as I really didn't want to know anymore. This was the first interaction that the two of us were having, and she'd chosen to ask me that? Alex was my boss, after all, and the thought of someone locking him in the basement seemed downright odd. The question made me think back on Alex's mood and behavior over the last few weeks. Upon arriving early to work on several occasions, I'd seen Alex already settled in his glassed-in corner office, sitting at his desk and looking very frazzled. I could still see him slumped over in his chair, sitting at his desk with an English muffin and a cup of coffee with a very disturbed look on his face. It was a very different looking Alex than the one that I was familiar with, and with this new information, I wondered if it had all had something to do with Ann.

I was thankful when the guys reappeared in the room and we left for dinner, as Ann had really made me feel uncomfortable. Dinner was uneventful, I have to say, but Ann seemed a bit withdrawn and not too involved in any conversation. At the end of the evening, Jerry and Alex made plans to attend a car show in eastern Pennsylvania for the following weekend and they invited me to join them. I wasn't sure that I wanted to go, but with some coaxing I agreed and the plans were put into place.

The following weekend, we all drove out to Hershey to walk the fairgrounds, looking at old antique cars that filled a large area. I had never been to a car show before, but I found it to be an interesting experience, to look at all of the old cars and learn about the vintage details. Alex and Jerry were huge fans of old cars, and Alex shared lots of information with me throughout the day. I mention this in particular because the attention that Alex paid to me may have made Ann a bit annoyed, as she went off to find a restroom and disappeared for about an hour or so. We all set out on a search to look for her after that, and she magically appeared just at the point of major frustration for the guys. Both men felt that she'd disappeared on purpose, and I sensed that there was something about Ann that they weren't sharing with me. At this point, they concluded the time at the car show and decided to head for home.

The ride home was very telling, as Ann seemed to be in a high state of agitation. Jerry and I were in the back seat attempting to have a nice conversation, but we kept getting interrupted by Ann. Ann was in the passenger's seat, nagging Alex about setting their wedding date and continuously repeating where and when they were going to be married. I found it to be strange behavior and Jerry made a few side comments to me about it, as well. I couldn't imagine that Alex was going to marry such a woman, as I thought there was something just not right about her. I was relieved when the long car ride was over and I was able to go off to the peace and quiet of my own home.

It was an interesting day, that one, but in my heart I knew that I was not interested in pursuing a relationship with Jerry. He was nice and had a great sense of humor, but he wasn't someone who I could see having a future with. Alex was encouraging the relationship between us, but I was starting to feel uncomfortable about how I was going to extract myself from the situation. However, before I knew what had happened, I was accepting an invitation to go for a Fourth of July weekend on Lake Erie; another date as a foursome. Alex arranged to pick me up at my apartment for the four-hour ride to the lake on a Friday afternoon. The plan was for me to ride along with him and Ann, and then proceed to Jerry's home where we would all stay.

To my surprise, that Friday afternoon Alex arrived at my home without Ann. I will never forget the way that Alex looked when I answered my door that particular day. I was already feeling quite anxious and had been prepared to leave hours prior to his arrival; I was considering calling and backing out at the last minute, though. I opened the door to see Alex standing in a pair of jeans and a dark navy polo that was covered with white granules of laundry detergent. The detergent matched the whiteness of his hair, as the specks stood out on the navy background of his shirt. The look on his face was one of blatant concern as he told me that Ann would not be joining us. He asked if we could talk for a few moments, so I invited him up the stairway and into my small kitchen.

Alex shared with me that he and Ann had had an argument earlier in the day, and that she had thrown her engagement ring at him and then dumped a box of detergent over his head. As I sat and listened to Alex talk about Ann, I couldn't imagine why someone would do such a thing to such a sweet man. The answer came a few moments later when he told me that Ann was bi-polar and that he'd recently found out that she hadn't been taking her medications. For some reason, I wasn't totally surprised by the revelation, as I of course had familiarity with such problems. Having dealt with someone with mental illness for my entire life, I had become quite adept at recognizing people who had such issues. I also realized that Alex was under a lot of stress as a result. He was a smoker, and I could see the number of cigarettes that he was smoking and the weight that he was losing as a result. He told me that his relationship with Ann was over, but that he was having a difficult time getting her to leave his home.

I don't remember giving Alex any advice in regards to his situation, but I do recall listening to the ordeal that he had been through. He had not been sleeping well, as he was afraid for his life. She had locked him in the basement and then gone after him with a knife. It seemed as though she had a habit of throwing things at him, and one of the items had been an iron. I had a lot of empathy for Alex because I knew how difficult it could be to live with someone that had no control over their emotions, and I felt sorry for him and his situation; notably, though, I also felt comfortable enough to share

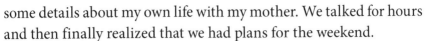

some details about my own life with my mother. We talked for hours and then finally realized that we had plans for the weekend.

Alex determined that Ann was not going to ruin his plans for the weekend, and he had no desire to go home and deal with her. He asked me if I would still like to go to the lake for the weekend and I agreed. The four-hour ride was the most revealing ride of my life, as we talked openly and freely with each other. I had never shared so much about myself with another person so easily, and I think that Alex felt the same way. I remember that there was a big full moon shining in the sky that evening, and the air felt sultry as we arrived at the lake close to midnight. We had arrived a lot later than Alex had initially planned, and he told me that he didn't want to wake up Jerry. I have to laugh about that now, as I later found out that Jerry was more of a night owl than either one of us.

Alex took me to a local winery where we had a bite to eat and some local wine. I wasn't much of a wine drinker, though, and before I knew it we were on the dance floor, slow dancing together. It offered a feeling of magic, as I felt very comfortable in his arms and he seemed to have the same feeling of ease. By this time, it was into the wee hours of the morning and I was wondering where we were going to spend the night. I didn't need to worry, though, as Alex took me to his sailboat that was moored at a local yacht club. We spent a very romantic evening together in the confines of his cozy sailboat. It was a different type of feeling than what I had ever experienced with anyone before, as I already knew that he cared about me.

The next morning, he got up early to go out and fetch us some breakfast sandwiches, as I was left to gain my bearings. We had not slept much the night before and now I had a few moments to collect my thoughts about the events of the prior day. My intuition had been correct about Alex, and the circumstances with Ann, as I'd perceived there was a problem. I wasn't sure how the rest of the weekend was going to play out, as I was supposed to be meeting up with Jerry, but although I didn't know what was going to happen next, I decided to just go with the flow of things.

As it turned out, I ended up being placed in the middle of both men for the weekend, as we met up with Jerry later in the morning. Alex didn't make mention of our arrival the previous night and the rest of the weekend was spent with my having the attention of both men. We went out on Jerry's boat and spent more time at the winery. It was a fun-filled weekend full of laughs and good times, and I felt comfortable throughout. It was Alex, however, who I was interested in, and on the car ride home we determined that we wanted to date. He assured me that he would talk to Jerry and let him know of our decision. Neither one of us felt that it would be a problem, believing that he would be happy for us. I had big concerns about Alex being my boss, though, and he still had issues in regards to dealing with Ann.

I will have to say that I was a bit embarrassed about that fact, that I was in the position of dating my boss, and so I had some real hesitancy. Going to work that following Monday morning was not easy for me. Though it weighed heavily on my mind, however, I knew that this was a bit different, in the fact that he was not married to Ann. I had a feeling that everything would work out for the best, but I wondered why things never came easily for me in regards to my romantic life. I remember calling off work one day during our dating, as I'd let my concerns get the best of me.

After the trip to the lake, Alex and I would secretly meet after work for dinner and or cocktails. We went out to restaurants or I would prepare something in my home, as we had some fear of being seen together. Alex would stay at my home for as long as possible and then return home to deal with Ann. He had asked her to leave and she was just not ready to let go of him. I will say that, at one point, I questioned whether or not he was being truthful with me, but I had no reason not to believe him. He assured me that he was sleeping in the guest room, and he even called me from his home to tell me that he was frightened of her and what she was doing. I understood his situation, as I knew what can happen when people need medication and the effect that it can have on their temperament. I felt helpless, though, and wondered how he was going to be able to get her out of his house. In many ways, I felt sorry for her and her disease.

It wasn't long until Ann figured out that Alex and I were seeing

each other, and that only made matters worse. She was an intelligent woman and somehow got ahold of my phone number, and so she then took to harassing me about my involvement with Alex. Ann was also threatening to call his boss to share the information about our dating relationship. We hadn't yet told human resources about our romantic involvement. We were so early in the dating process that we hadn't actually shared our relationship with anyone, and yet we already knew that our secret was about to become scandalous. Alex was a vice president in the organization – I reported to him and he determined my bonuses.

Our rendezvous after work were taking place on a daily basis, and we suspected that our co-workers in the office were becoming aware of our attraction for each other, so Alex determined that it was time to notify his boss and also the CEO of the company. I am sure that it was a difficult conversation to have, as I was one of his direct reports. His bosses were not too thrilled about the news, but because we were both single and good employees, it seemed to be alright. Alex even got the okay for us to attend the big annual formal together so that he could bring me as his date, and in retrospect, that was our coming out party, so to speak.

Attending the formal was an awkward evening for me, as I felt all eyes were on the two of us. It was our first public outing as a couple, and I'm sure it sent the rumor mill into full force. It was after that event that several of my female co-workers made a visit to the human resources department to complain that I was getting large bonuses as a result of my sleeping with the boss. I had always received large bonuses in the past, though, and if the truth were to be known, I actually for the first time got smaller bonuses. Still, the complaints created a problem for me and for Alex, as he was summoned to speak with the CEO.

The CEO wasn't happy with the circumstances and the reports that he was getting from human resources, and Alex was feeling the pressure, as he was also trying to get Ann to move out of his home and she was still threatening him with calls to his boss. He could hardly get any work done, as she was calling his work number nonstop and threatening him. He finally figured out who her psychiatrist was and that they had prescribed medications she wasn't taking. Ann was getting progressively more dangerous too, with threats of bodily harm to Alex and to herself. Their engagement had long since ended, but she was still hanging onto him in hopes that their marriage would take place. Meanwhile, Alex was going back and forth with the psychiatrist in regards to her medications, but Ann would no longer speak with the psychiatrist and was essentially just refusing to take her medications. The psychiatrist finally relented to having her committed, as he saw no other opportunity to help her. It seemed to me that fate was finally on our side in helping to get her out of his home.

It was when Alex had tolerated three days of her screaming and yelling in his home, along with items being hurled at him, that the psychiatrist tired of the conversations and antics, and finally wrote the order for her to be committed. Two ambulances and three squad cars arrived at his home and removed her as she kicked and screamed the entire time. Alex relayed to me that she'd had to be restrained, and that all of the neighbors converged in his driveway to watch the spectacle. He found it all to be very embarrassing, as he is a very private individual. Despite his best efforts, though, they finally found out was happening in his home and what he had been going through.

Not only had Alex been dealing with Ann, but he was getting grief from his staff members that were unhappy as a result of our dating. The CEO had indicated to Alex that they needed to get this issue taken care of, as he was tired of the reports. I wasn't aware of these discussions with the CEO until later on, but it turned out that they had made a decision to move me out of the department.

It was a surprise to me, as I was summoned to the human resources department and told that I was receiving a promotion to a new position that was being created. I was going to be based in Pittsburgh, but I would be travelling all over the country to meet with brokers and bankers to promote a new product line. In essence, I was getting a promotion, and I couldn't believe my ears. I was instructed to collect all of my things out of my office at the end of the day and to relocate them to another building where my office would be set up. I was also not permitted to share the information with anyone in my office, or to share my whereabouts, and that included the office manager.

I really didn't know how to feel when I left the human resources office that day. In one respect, I knew that I had been a bad girl for having an affair with the boss, but at the same time I was somewhat ashamed of receiving a promotion that came complete with a brand new car. I'd doubled my income, but I had also worked many years for the company and had been overlooked for positions on many occasions in the past when I had applied for such positions – even ones that I was over-qualified for! In some respect, I felt that I had earned that promotion and was very deserving of it even though it was all unexpected; I just hadn't planned for it to happen in just this way, as I certainly hadn't been looking to better myself through a relationship. It had all just happened, as though it had been laid out by someone greater than myself. I realized that Alex and I could now be together, though, as all of these things had been taken care of and it all seemed as if it was meant to be.

Throughout my life, I'd often wondered how I was going to meet someone and get married. I think most women wonder how it is going to happen for them. I would never have imagined that my love story would have evolved in the way that it did, truth be told. In my heart, I thought that someone would come to my rescue and that I would be the one saved. It wasn't until years after our marriage that I really thought about it, and realized that I was the one who had rescued my husband from a bad situation. Somehow, that had long escaped my awareness. I knew that Alex had been through a lot in regards to Ann and that she'd absolutely frightened him, but in spite of all that he was going through, he was able to show me how much he loved me and that he was committed to me.

After Ann was released from the hospital, Alex helped her to get situated back in the city in which she'd grown up. Alex had asked me to marry him two months after our first date on Lake Erie, even though it wasn't to be official for a while, as all of these things had to work themselves out. After Ann was situated in her new place, though, I moved in with Alex in December of 1994 and we were married at the end of January of 1995. We celebrated our first Christmas together in his home and made plans for a small wedding with a few family and friends. Our wedding day was bittersweet for me, as my parents had already left for their annual Florida vacation and wouldn't be present on my actual wedding day.

Our wedding took place in our home, and we were surrounded by close friends, my sister May, and my brother Martin. On the morning of my wedding, my parents called from Florida to wish us well on our wedding day and to apologize for not staying in town to see me get married. I was sorry that I hadn't waited for their return, but we really didn't want to wait. We had discussed getting married by a justice of the peace and just having my parents attend, but decided otherwise. Upon their return in April, we had a wedding reception at a local hotel banquet room to which we invited family and friends to join us in celebrating our marriage.

Our honeymoon plans were parlayed, as well, because of the passing of Alex's father. Several days prior to leaving on a ski trip to Colorado, we got the sad news. Instead of going to Colorado, we went to Illinois to attend his funeral. I got to meet all of Alex's family members and it was a memorable moment for me, as I met all five brothers and sisters as well as his mother. I couldn't believe how well they all got along, and it was really only then that I realized that I myself had been part of a dysfunctional family. I had never met a family that got along so well together and truly loved and accepted each other despite any shortcomings. What was more amazing was how they immediately accepted me into their family with love and affection. The occasion was a sad one for their family, but the way they all dealt with the passing of their father was admirable.

Alex and I finally took our honeymoon in April of 1995, when we went to Hilton Head Island and then a month later headed off to the Greek Isles. I was being sent there on a business trip and Alex accompanied me, so it was as though we got to have two honeymoons. I truly believe that Alex was meant to be my soulmate, and that our

meeting was destined in the grand scheme of things, so the extra celebrations only seemed to be warranted.

In January of 2017, we will have been married for twenty-two years. As with most marriages, we have had our good times and our bad times, but I know in my heart that God placed the right man in my life. I was attracted to Alex partly because of his balanced personality, and there are no surprises to that effect when I arrive home at the end of the day. He is very much like my father in this, way and he is honored to know that they have had such qualities in common.

I entered marriage knowing that I had dysfunction in my genes and a lot of baggage that I carried with me, and it certainly made me wonder how things would turn out. Through the difficult times, I admit I have sometimes felt like bolting out the door, but thankfully I have had enough sense to realize that any of our marital blemishes can be turned to bliss in moments. I find myself to be fortunate in having an understanding partner who knows how to take care of my scarred soul.

Moving Forward

If my entire life could have become defined by just one moment, it would have been the moment when my father passed away. I say this because that's the moment when it became apparent to me that I realized that everything which I knew in respect to my family had been held together by one person, and that one person had been my father. He was the glue of our family, and it was after his passing that it all started to unravel.

I was forty years old at the time and at a possible midpoint in my own life. I had been married to Alex for only a few years, and I had already met his entire family, witnessing how his brothers and sisters related to each other, and seeing that it was very different from the way in which we all related to one another. But this became more evident once my father suffered his stroke, as I was placed in the positon of having responsibility for my mother. It happened so suddenly that none of us were prepared for what would happen to our family.

The last time that I saw my father in his full capacity was at the grand opening of my new business. He had attended along with my mother, and my brother Martin and his new wife. May and William were unable to attend that day, but I was very happy, as my newly designed shop was filled with lots of activity and I had hired a band, so there was lots of great food and conversation. I was busy talking with everyone and not really paying much attention to any one person in particular, though I was aware of the presence of my father, and he seemed to want to speak with me – he just had that look about him. We'd had so very little time in the last few weeks to really talk with

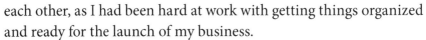

each other, as I had been hard at work with getting things organized and ready for the launch of my business.

He had made a few trips in to visit with me, but I'd always been so anxious to get back to what I'd been doing, as I had a list of priorities a mile long. Had I only paid more attention to him during those visits... but I never imagined that my father's life would end so suddenly. He had been such an active man that I thought he would live well into his nineties, at least. I thought my mother would leave this earth prior to him, as she was much more sedentary and had all of the health issues.

Nevertheless, the day that he had his stroke would remain etched in my mind forever. I had not spoken to him since my grand opening, and at least a week that had passed me by since then. It wasn't a common practice for me to go for such a long period of time without talking with him, as there used to be a daily phone call every evening between us, just to check in. I remember that I tried to call him on the morning of his stroke, and my mother said that he was out in the garden working. That's where a neighbor found him about an hour after my call, there laying on the ground. I wish that she would have gone out and gotten him, and maybe he would have been found sooner. I don't blame her, of course, as that's the way that things were set up to happen, I have to think.

It was almost surreal that only a few hours later I was rushing out of my store to their small community hospital, only to see him just prior to his being loaded on the life flight helicopter. He was being transferred to a major hospital in the city, as they didn't have the type of care that he needed for his massive stroke. I was in tears as he waved goodbye to us and I was unaware that this would be his last really conscious moment. Everyone made it, to see him off on that flight, except for William.

From the local hospital, we all headed into the city to a larger hospital, and we were met by a neurosurgeon who gave us some very grim news. He shared with us that our father had had a very bloody stroke, and that he needed to operate or he would die. They neglected to tell us that on the helicopter they had already lost him and revived him. As a family, we agreed to have the surgeon operate in an attempt to save his life, and with no real thought of the consequences. We knew that he was an active man and would never want to live as an invalid or a burden to anyone else, but it seemed like the only option.

The surgeon did warn us that he might lose some capabilities as a result of the surgery, but he also needed to leave immediately to perform the surgery, as time was precious. We'd never had to make such an important decision before as a family, and my parents had no papers in place to guide us in our decision making. My mother was in such a state of shock that she barely said anything, as she seemed to be somewhere else. Without much hesitation or thought, we all agreed for the surgeon to proceed.

The hospital was close to my business, so I agreed to have my mother come and live with me so that she could be nearby. My business had barely been open for two weeks when all of this took place, but I needed to pay attention to the care of my father as well as the care of my mother. Ironically, after the surgery, the surgeon took a leave of absence for several weeks, and any attempt to talk with him about my father's future was useless.

For the next two months, I took my mother to the hospital every day to sit with him, and I would stay with them both for as long as possible. I would run over to the store to check on things and then leave to go back to the hospital to make sure my mother had lunch and to check on my father. I really couldn't concentrate on my business at all, and so I left everything in the hands of my new employees. I was very thankful later on that I had hired a few angels who were able to be responsible enough to handle things in my absence. I spent a lot of my upfront cash that I had available for their time and help, but my mind was obviously somewhere else. I had a lot on my shoulders, as I was spending every moment at the hospital, somewhat managing a new business, and also taking care of my mother in making sure all of her needs were being met. I was also spending a lot of my time talking aloud and pleading to God to spare the life of my father, as I wasn't ready to lose him from my life.

I felt frustrated and sometimes abandoned as I watched my father lay motionless in his hospital bed. My brothers and sister lived at such a far distance from the hospital that it became difficult for them to be there on such a regular basis. My brother Martin especially had a difficult time seeing our father in such a state, so that he stayed away for weeks before reappearing. William surprisingly made regular visits in to visit with him. Meanwhile, I wondered if my father would ever recover and, as the days wore on, I didn't understand the implications for his future.

One day at the hospital, a member of the nursing staff pulled me aside and told me that I needed to move on with my life. She asked me what I did for a living and then she told me that I needed to go and tend to my business. I was appalled that she would say such a thing to me, as my hope for my father's recovery was endless. Thinking back, I now realize that it was her way of telling me that there was no hope. I didn't listen to her, of course, and I continued to carry on with my daily routine of taking myself and my mother to the hospital. My siblings were able to visit on weekends and they called me continuously to find out the status of my father's condition, but I never really had anything positive to report – he'd made no improvements. My other family members were seemingly able to carry on with their daily routines without too much disruption. I knew that it didn't mean that they didn't care, but I seemed to be the one who was called upon to carry that load at that time in my life.

I simply didn't want to believe that my father was going to die. He was a man of such great strength, courage, and resilience that I thought he would bounce back. I was very defiant in my thoughts about his recovery, in spite of all the evidence pointing otherwise. It was a conversation that I had one day with Martin which would cause me to spiral out of control, as we would debate my father's very existence.

Martin called me one afternoon about a month after my father's surgery, while I was in my shop and catching up on some things, my mother being at the hospital. He painted a very dim picture of my father's life as an invalid and his life in a rehabilitation center, as he wouldn't be able to come home. He pointed out the inability of my mother or any other family member to take care of him. I remember being very angry with Martin and, in my anger, screaming and crying about his giving up hope for our father's recovery. Thinking back, I know that I probably frightened my staff at the shop, as I lost control of my emotions and cried for a long time after that conversation ended. I was in disbelief at what I thought was a cold phone call from my own brother. I somehow was able to forgive him for being so blunt and realistic with me, later on, but it wasn't easy. Facing the hard facts of life can be extremely painful, and that was the lesson that I was learning. I was mad at the world, simply enough, as things were not going the way that I wanted them to.

I was so mad at Martin, though, that the next morning I found myself all alone at my father's bedside, behaving as though it was a confessional room. I told him how mad I was at my brother and that I couldn't understand his way of thinking. I hope that both my father and my brother will forgive me for doing such a thing, and I pray that my father didn't hear what I had to say or hear the sound of the waterfall that fell from my eyes. I am ashamed of myself for doing such a thing, but my father was always so good at listening to me – and I wanted it all to be alright.

Unfortunately, things were not going to be as I wanted them to be. Eight weeks after the surgery, the neurosurgeon finally returned from his leave and called our family together for a meeting. I was pleased that William showed up for that meeting; in the weeks prior to my father's stroke, William and my father had been spending a lot of time together. Looking back, I know that my father had an inkling that his time on earth was short, as he was seeking out all of his children. I was surprised on a couple of occasions that William and my father arrived at my shop together to take me to breakfast or go to lunch. Now, it makes me happy to know that my brother and my father were on good terms at that point, and that they had some time to spend together. I know that my father had worked hard on staying in touch with him, as he loved him very much.

Our meeting and discussion with the neurosurgeon was a serious one, as he told us that it was time to consider placing my father under the care of hospice. He had not fully recovered consciousness, and

any hope for him to have any function or quality of life was moot. The doctor told us that it was time for us to tell him goodbye. At that moment, all the hope that I'd had for my father's recovery came crashing down around me. I realized that my father was just a shell which remained amongst us, and I prayed that his body was no longer suffering and that his soul had been released from our earthly boundaries. With my husband by my side, I went to his bedside to tell him how much I loved him, and what a great father that he had been to me.

Later that same day, they moved my father to a local hospice. I wasn't really sure what a hospice was, as I had never encountered one before, but our experience with them was very caring and compassionate as they tended to my father and the well-being of our family. They talked with each one of our family members separately to see how we were coping and offer any assistance. Instead of taking my mother to the hospital every day, we were now going to the hospice to visit him.

They kept my father injected with morphine and they assured us that he was pain free. It took a week for him to pass, and I felt comfortable, as he was no longer connected to the tubes and gadgets that he'd been connected to in the trauma unit. I was happy that he was in a homelike environment for his passing, as compared to a cold and sterile hospital room.

Dealing with my father's passing was the most difficult time of my life. He had been such a wonderful role model, despite the hardships that he endured. After his passing, I needed to go on antidepressants, as I had no sense of closure in regards to his death. I moped around my shop for weeks even though I knew that my father would not have wanted me to behave in such a manner; I couldn't help myself, though. As some comfort, I was happy that I had my business to keep my mind occupied.

It wasn't until I had a dream approximately three months after my father's death that I was able to really move on with my life. I saw my father very distinctly, sitting in a chair with a smile on his face and giving me the okay sign with his fingers. The dream was very simple and memorable, and upon waking from that dream, I knew that my father was in a better place and that everything was okay. The heaviness that I had been carrying around with me seemed to disappear almost instantaneously, and I felt like I could smile again.

Not only did I have that dream which signified that he was okay, but I started finding heart shapes in the strangest of places – ones that I felt were some sort of a sign he was giving to me. Some people say that they receive "pennies from heaven" when a loved one who's passed is around them, but for me it was heart shapes. The hearts started to appear on the day of my father's funeral, and to this day I will find them occasionally. Let me tell you how it began... On the day prior to the funeral, my husband and I decided to stay in a hotel near the location of our family home. My brother and sister had each invited us to spend the night in their homes, but for some reason I wanted my privacy and wanted to give them theirs. The morning of his funeral, I woke up and, the moment that I placed my feet on the floor, I took notice of several very small confetti hearts all over the floor beside my bed. They were brightly colored and sprinkled around the floor as though they'd dropped from heaven. I hadn't noticed them the previous day or evening and, as weird as it may seem, I felt that they'd somehow been placed there by my father.

On another occasion, I was having an extremely difficult day in my shop and was feeling very disheartened about a few things. When I left my shop at the end of the day to get into my car, I saw that someone had drawn a large heart on the back of my car window in the newly fallen snow. There were numerous heart sightings in the most unconventional of ways that arrived in the most timeliest of moments in the early years after his passing. They're not as prominent now, but when they do show up, I still feel that they are from my father and that he is sending me his love.

I don't know if my brothers or sisters received any signs from above, but I knew that if my father was watching over us, his first concern would have been my mother. I know that my father worried about what would happen to her, and I made a promise to him on his deathbed that I would make sure that she would be taken care of. I have not been able to live up to that promise to the extent that I promised, but I have been involved in her care. My sister lived a mile down the road from my mother and father, and so most of her care fell into her hands and those of Martin, who lived right next door.

My mother and father lived in an apartment on Martin's property, as he had built it for my parents to spend their retirement years. My parents had actually lived with Martin for a short period of time, but things changed when Martin got married to his third wife. The apartment that my parents had shared now housed only my mother; she had been so dependent on my father for almost everything, to the point of her nearly acting like an invalid even though she was fully capable of doing everything for herself. I don't mean to sound mean in regards to my mother, but she really pushed my father's buttons, and I hate to even say this, but she may have even caused him the stress that led to his stroke. She was constantly demanding that he do things for her, asking him to do everything for her.

Once she was left alone, the same type of scenario started to play out with my brother and my sister due to their proximity and her demanding nature. She became dependent on them for all of her needs, and this was when the problems really started. The trouble became apparent to me when I made a visit to my mother's home a couple of weeks after the funeral. I had taken a day off work to drive the two and a half hours to their home, but only to receive an earful from Martin. He approached me as I got out of my car and immediately told me that I didn't come to visit anymore, and that I'd neglected everyone. Once again, I was taken aback by my brother's bluntness, and his comments were very hurtful. He then told me that he had things to do, and that he didn't have any time to spend with me.

I had not seen myself as being neglectful, as I had been working hard to recover some losses that I had taken in my new business and was spending long hours trying to make it a success, so I didn't understand Martin's reaction to me and could only try to not let it bother me. I went into the apartment to visit with my mother then, and the complaining started immediately – about how she wasn't getting everything that she needed on a daily basis. I couldn't imagine that to be true, as she had both Martin and May to purchase the things that she needed. She told me, though, that May was not stopping to see her every day, and that Martin was only going to the store once a week. I asked her what she could possibly need from a store on a daily basis, and reminded her that they both had employment responsibilities. I knew that her expectations from her children were high, and that she was probably lonely and wanted some companionship, but I felt like I was her sounding board and was now being placed in the middle of Martin and May. I didn't like the position my mother was putting me in, but I felt my mother was looking to me to help resolve some issues she saw in regards to her care.

I have to share this with you because a great divide was about to take place in reaction to the care of my mother, and the fallout between family members would split our family apart for many years to come. I also have to add that my mother played her part in pitting us all against each other, as she was thinking only about herself. My mother was very demanding of both Martin and May, and it was wearing thin for both of them. I heard it from all angles and I tried my best to stay out of any friction that was taking place, even attempting to help the situation by taking my mother to live with me for a week at a time on a regular basis. She wasn't happy being away from her own home, though, and she didn't like sitting in my shop all day, as she then couldn't watch her soap operas. I finally set up a television in my shop so that she could watch her shows – and she still complained.

Trying to please my mother could be a difficult endeavor, but we all tried in our own ways to make her happy. My sister also knew that my mother was lonely, so she decided to purchase her a cat to keep her company. One wouldn't think that a cat could cause such disharmony, but it actually led to major problems since Martin's wife didn't like animals of any type and refused to step into my mother's home as a result. She had such a distaste for animals, in fact, that she didn't want any animals on her property! I don't believe that my sister purchased the cat to intentionally cause problems, but that is exactly what it did. Martin and May got into such a squabble over the cat that May moved my mother out of her apartment and into her own home. She did all of this against my better judgement, as I knew how my mother could be, but my sister felt that it would ultimately make her life easier. I couldn't imagine the life that my sister and her husband would have as a result, but her husband seemed to be alright with the decision.

On the day that my sister moved my mother out of her apartment, there was quite a battle between my sister and her husband and Martin and his wife. I am glad that I wasn't present, as supposedly the screaming and yelling could be heard all through the small community. The neighbors got quite an earful, and it was the talk of the town. Unfortunately, that major confrontation caused May and Martin not to speak to each other again for over ten years. Martin was no longer invited to any of the family get-togethers at my sister's house, and as a result, my two nephews didn't have their uncle around to see them grow up.

It was sad to see the two of them so at odds with each other, as they only lived a mile apart. May and Martin were not the only two that would not speak for years, though. Martin and William also had a falling out over the ownership of tools. William was always selling his personal tools to come up with some fast cash, and Martin or my father were always the ones that helped him out. Ultimately William would always come back and want to buy them back at a later date. After my father passed, Martin and William got into a debate over some tools and, as a result, they also stopped speaking to each other. They have fought over toys and tools for most of their lives and, sadly, it finally caused a permanent rift between the two of them.

William's need for money not only caused a problem with him and Martin, but led to a problem with my mother. Shortly after my mother moved in with May, he arrived to visit with her one day and, when my mother came to the door, she didn't recognize him, he had changed his hair so much. His point for the visit was only to ask for his portion of his inheritance. My mother refused to give him any money and, as a result, she didn't see or hear from her son again for the next eighteen years. It is also possible that he was terribly offended that his own mother didn't recognize him. After my father's passing, her doctor had placed my mother on some different medications and they seemed to affect her memory pretty severely. They finally took her off of them and she recovered her normal sharpness, but at that time, they may have influenced at least one damaged relationship.

During that change of medication, my mother's memory became an issue for my sister, as well. I know that May struggled with the care of my mother, as May would arrive home to find the temperature in her home at well over 95 degrees. My mother would have turned the thermostat to the highest level possible. I tried hard to help out as much as possible and would take my mother for a week or so to give her a break, but it became more difficult when we moved to Ohio. My husband had retired and I'd sold my business after five years of ownership, and in January of 2002 we moved to our second home in Ohio. The distance became a barrier, and I also decided to take a job as an interior designer that kept me very busy. We were also trying to enjoy my husband's retirement years by spending our winters in Florida.

The distance from my family became even greater, and I am sure that it sometimes angered my sister that I wasn't able to take my mother as often. I will admit at times that there was some tension between May and I in regards to the care of my mother during that timeframe. I cared about what happened and often felt guilty, but I also felt that it had not been my decision to so fully take on the responsibility of my mother, as May had. Both of my brothers were also relieved of any responsibility, as they had not been involved in any decision making in regards to her care. I stayed in touch with all of them, as I was the one that relayed information about each of us from one to the other. I even wrote all of them letters, asking that we could all get along. The letters were basically ignored, though, and after a period of time I just gave up on any hope of my family ever reconciling.

I tried my best to help my sister by taking my mother with my husband and I to Florida on our yearly getaway. I had the flexibility with my job to take three months off in the wintertime to go to Florida, and so I would take my mother with us for several weeks. My sister and her husband would then travel to Florida to pick her up and spend some time with us. It was always an adventure to pick my mother up from my sister's home and place her in the back seat with the large collie dog that I had at the time. I have to give a lot of credit to my husband for the patience that he displayed in helping to care for her on those trips. We were leading an active lifestyle, and leaving my mother in the Florida condo alone at times became worrisome to the point that it filled me with anxiety. She wasn't interested in doing anything but watching television and sitting in a comfy chair.

I was trying hard to enjoy our trip, but the responsibility of making sure my mother was taking her medications was stressful in itself. I often left her alone in the condo since she really didn't have much interest in going to the beach or with us on our golf outings, but I worried about what might happen while I was out enjoying myself. By the time my sister arrived to enjoy her time in Florida, my mother was more than ready to go back home. One time she even had her bags packed and ready to go several days in advance. My mother was really dependent on my sister, more than anyone, and she would tell me often that she really didn't like her trips to Florida. Much as I tried hard to make her time with us as enjoyable as possible by playing cards, games, going out to dinner, and taking her shopping, it was really difficult for her to be out of her normal routine, as she was happy with her lifestyle. And yet, the times that she spent with my husband and I in Florida were some of the most enjoyable moments that I spent with her, despite some of my concerns. In spite of it all, we had some good times laughing together.

As my mother got into her early eighties, it became too difficult for my sister to take care of her, and the trips to Florida likewise ended. Conversations started to lean towards what we should do with her, as she was making life difficult for my sister and her husband. It finally got to the point where she had an episode and landed back in a mental institution. I went back to Pennsylvania to help my sister in making some decisions in regards to her care, and it was at this point that we decided that, once she was discharged, we would immediately place her in an assisted living community. We gave it much thought and found a place that would accept her as a resident, even with all of her problems.

I don't really remember the reason for the breakdown that specific time, but it brought things to the forefront in our needing to move her to a community. We found a place that we thought that she would like, and it wasn't a secured unit for memory impaired individuals. Some of the places that we'd looked at, we just couldn't imagine as environments that could make my mother happy. We found an assisted living community, though, that would accept her and which we thought would work well, and so we went ahead and made the arrangements. My mother, of course, was not happy when she found out, but she really had no choice in the matter. We got her situated in a small unit and, surprisingly, she adjusted quite well. She seemed to like her independence and all of the activities that they offered. She socialized with the other residents, and the community probably offered some her happier times since my father had passed away. There were some paranoid episodes that took place, I admit; however, the facility was very helpful in dealing with the few occasions on which they occurred. She had spent seven years living with my sister, and I commend my sister and brother–in–law for giving up a lot of their freedom to take care of my mother. I adore my brother-in-law for his patience in dealing with my mother, as well, and for the kindness and understanding he showed toward her – as I am sure she could be difficult.

And meanwhile, my husband and I learned from everything, and continued moving forward. For our part, we realized that we had passions for helping seniors and for trying to make a difference as they moved through such difficult times as my mother has faced since my father passed. Eventually, through our interactions with those who were struggling in different ways, we both became advocates for seniors in need.

My life has been filled with lots of struggles to overcome, and I look at each battle scar as a reminder of the wars I have fought.

The lessons that I have learned have only helped me to make me the person that I am today. I hope that I can use my life experiences to help others as we make this journey together, and I will say that keeping my faith and hope in a power greater than that of myself has helped me to overcome my difficulties.

Moving forward in regards to my family... at the time of this writing, my siblings have not all reconciled their differences. I have prayed for years that we would all reunite and make peace with each other, and through the years, I have kept in touch with each of them on an individual basis and provided them with information about each other – in hopes that something would spur them to reconnect.

Martin and May have forgiven each other, and talk and visit with each other without involving their spouses. They both visit my mother frequently, as she is now living in a skilled nursing facility and is confined to a wheelchair. We are happy that she is receiving good care and seems to enjoy all of the activities and the attention that she receives. She is still on the demanding side, as she tells the staff how to take care of her needs, but I'm actually happy that she's that way because, as a result, she won't let anyone take advantage of her and her situation.

My sister and I, in a recent conversation, spoke of how we feel that it's such a shame that she suffered from her disease, because she would have been quite an impressive lady had she not been blemished in this way. I really enjoy the time that I am able to spend with her on my visits to see her, and I love her very much.

At the time of this writing, I have to say that it has been confirmed to me that prayers really do get answered, as one that I had been praying for a long time finally got answered. I had pretty much given up any hope and was totally surprised by the call which brought the news. My brother and my mother finally saw each other for the first time in eighteen years when he made a visit to the nursing home to see her. The day that William called me to tell me that he made that visit was a remarkable day. I was overjoyed with the news, and happy that they were able to reconcile and that my brother had been able to forgive and let go of whatever indifference he'd been holding inside of himself.

I was also relieved that I wasn't going to have the difficult conversation with him that I'd expected in this regard, as he was planning to visit my home with his wife of five years who I hadn't yet met. I hadn't been thrilled with the thought of his visit, knowing that I may not be able to hold in my thoughts regarding his behavior toward our mother. Over the years, I had called and literally begged him to go visit her, as she'd almost died several times, and I knew that she longed to see him. But, news of their conversation took away any reservations I'd had, and I was finally able to simply look forward to seeing him and meeting his new wife.

During William's visit to our home recently, I learned that he'd held some resentment and that there'd been some sibling jealousy that played a part in his behavior in regards to his family members. His new wife has been a great influence in helping him to overcome some of his negative thoughts and feelings, and I am happy he has found such a soulmate. I know that her role in his life is one that has been a most influential one, in a positive way, and I am grateful to her for the role. During their visit, I also learned about some of the real difficulties in my brother's previous marriages, and realized that there are always two sides to every story. Which side of the story is true and what really happened, I am still not sure, but William is my brother and he is the one who is in my life. As to whether or not my brothers and sisters ever reunite with each other, that remains to be seen. I have decided to not interfere, and that if it is to be in God's grand plan, then in due time it will happen. In the meantime, I will continue to pray for each of them to find it in their heart to forgive and forget, as life is far too short for holding grudges.

I always laugh at the saying that says, "You can pick your friends but you cannot pick your family members." I love each and every one of my family members, and if I could choose any differently, I would not change a thing.

My Life Tutorial

Looking back on my entire life, I sometimes wonder how I survived and came out on the other side without having broken apart or imploded somewhere along the way. Remembering the incident in the chicken coop seemed to be an important moment for me, as it set off a wave of introspective thoughts. And remembering the event was startling enough in and of itself, as it gave me a new awareness about my family relationships and the fact that my body had been wrongly abused by someone at such a young age.

Strangely, throughout my adulthood, I thought more about my mother's words than I thought about the act itself. I was in my twenties when I recalled the event, and the word "damaged" kept ringing through my head. I knew she meant that I was "damaged" in a physical way, as I was no longer a virgin. My mother grew up in a time when losing your virginity was a major event, and you saved yourself for marriage. I, on the other hand, was living in a time when some of my fellow classmates graduated from high school while single and pregnant. I grew up in a small town, and it seemed to be commonplace at the time, so I was able to justify in my mind that the single event wasn't going to define who I was as a person; I told myself that I would not let the knowledge of it affect any physical relationships I might have, and I still looked forward to meeting someone of the opposite sex and having that type of relationship.

As an adult, I thought more about the possible emotional damage I may have sustained, as I thought more about my mother's words than the act itself. However, in thinking about my mother's mental condition at the time and the actual situation, I think it was physical damage that she was more concerned about. Over the years, I most often questioned why it took me so long to remember, and I wondered if there was anything else that was going to rear its ugly head – thus, emotional damage was my central concern.

Throughout my entire life, during my moments of self-doubt, I would ask myself why I felt that way and wonder if there was a connection. I would rifle through self-help books for the answer to my wavering lack of confidence and my shyness. I finally found that being too absorbed in my own self-reflection was more harmful than helpful, though. Instead of turning inward, I decided to turn outward and focus on helping other people. As a result, I found that I had a passion for helping senior citizens, and the more that I gave of myself in this way, the more confident that I felt. I was better able to manage my dark thoughts and I was better able to keep the light in. I also found it easier to make and keep friends, as I was no longer so absorbed in my own concerns.

In overcoming my personal struggles, I made a personal commitment to not let my past spoil my current relationships. As you can imagine, growing up with a mentally ill parent had been very challenging, and left me and my family with scars that may never go away. Unfortunately, the world is filled with families who have very similar types of hurdles with loved ones and family members who may suffer with mental illness. And sadly, such diseases are too often just swept under the carpet with the hope that they will just go away. As a child, I knew that it was something that I was embarrassed to confess to anyone, and sometimes to this day, I often hate to admit that it is part of my family genealogy. For me, it has been related to the fear of being judged, as to what others might think about my own state of mind.

It was during my high school years when I was most focused on covering up my mother's illness and trying to hide our family situation from everyone who I knew, and I really didn't give much thought to how it affected me personally. High school can be challenging enough if you are a little bit different, and it can be even tougher if you add on a stigma of some sort. I am always saddened to hear about a teenager or a young person who took their own life as a result of bullying, or from simply not fitting in with their peers. It makes me wonder what happened in their life that made them break, and why someone wasn't there to help them.

I sometimes think about how nice it would have been to have had some guidance from an outside source in helping me to deal with what was happening in my home and school. I internalized so many of my concerns and worries that I thought that they were hidden from the rest of the world. With this being said, though, I also think back about the signs that should have been recognizable. I kept so much locked up inside of me, as I was extremely shy, which was a marker for low self-confidence, and I spent endless hours in my room alone, experiencing difficulties with feeling comfortable about revealing my own thoughts.

I am not sure what my parents may have thought about me, as they knew I was a little different in comparison to May and her busy social schedule. As an adult, looking back at my high school years, I felt robbed of my youth due to my relationship with Mr. Santini, and I also attributed some bouts of depression to having that relationship. During my twenties, I had overwhelming feelings of guilt, as I knew that something was not normal or ethical in respect to our relationship, and it also hampered my capabilities to have normal relationships with boys and young men of my own age.

For most of my high school years, I felt like an outcast since I felt different than my classmates. It's now obvious to me that my high school years were somewhat painful in many respects, and my twenties didn't get any easier. My twenties were very significant years for me in regards to my personal growth, though, and they are years that I would not want to go back and live over. However, they did serve me as a big turning point in regards to how I looked at life, and most importantly, how I perceived myself. Being a rather introspective soul, I can be overly critical of myself, and it was in those years that that critical part came reeling to the surface and made me question who I really was, deep in my core.

Thinking back, I realize that it all started at the very moment when I remembered what had happened to me in my childhood. But it was the experience of living with the other girls in that small apartment that summer, and the stark differences in personality, which really brought to the forefront how introverted and withdrawn I was. I had a difficult time relating to the other girls, as I tended to isolate myself from the others; the girls surrounding me were all going out every night to party and have fun, and I constantly asked myself why I couldn't let myself join in and go out with them in the evenings. I didn't know what I was so afraid of, and it made me feel very lonely.

Yet, it was also this same group of girls who I later witnessed as being very cruel toward Monica, the victim of AIDS, and that sickened my soul. I had seen mean girls on the playground before and maybe at one time I might have been a mean girl myself toward someone, as children can sometimes be cruel. But prior to going to New Jersey, I had never seen such vicious behavior toward anyone who happened to be different, and particularly to someone who was deathly ill.

The summer in New Jersey was an eye opener for me, as it changed me in so many ways and made me realize that I have a wonderful family in spite of our challenges. I discovered that I could love my family with all of my heart and still maintain my independence. My return to my home after that summer made me happy to be back in a community with familiar roots, as I saw how the world can sometimes be brutal. As a result of that summer away from home, I found a deeper appreciation for my family in spite of our problems. It did not mean that I would stay with them forever, as I had different goals for my life, but I knew that I could always come home to people who loved and cared about me.

It was during that summer that I also came to terms with accepting my mother and her illness. My perception changed, as I now knew that she had no control over her illness and that it controlled her. I watched Monica struggle without any support from her family, left to deal with her disease on her own. It was obvious that her family didn't care about her and I decided that I didn't want to be that type of person.

I had taken off from my home earlier that summer in such a way that it may have appeared that I didn't care about the people who I'd left behind, as I'd just wanted to escape. Now, though, I decided that I did not want to be the type of person who left blemishes and open wounds on the trail behind them, as I really did care. It also made me realize that I wanted to be as supportive of my father as I possibly could.

As supportive as my father was to me and my future plans, though, I still questioned myself. It was in my late twenties when I began to question whether or not I could possibly be like my mother and have her illness. I knew that my thinking might have been a bit distorted as to what was normal, as a result of my upbringing. These types of thoughts were especially disturbing and could be quite strong when I was drinking heavily or doing something that went against my moral upbringing, and I found that drinking alcohol only promoted my feelings of heaviness, and made me have feelings of low self-worth. The more that I drank, the more my periods of darkness would appear.

It was in the midst of the dark moment after the loss of my unborn child that I had a revelation that life is solely what you make of it. I knew that I could continue to feel sorry for myself and my circumstances, or I could pull myself up and try to make the best of things. Thus, it was in my darkest hour that I found the strength and courage to persevere, and decided to depend on myself for my own success. I made the decision to stop using alcohol as a way to escape my problems, and the periods of depression and my heavy thoughts lightened as a result. I also gained confidence in myself and renewed my self-image. I knew in my heart that it was through the grace of God that I was finally able to move forward in a positive direction.

Moving forward was sometimes not easy for me, as it felt more like sidestepping since it seemed like a long time that I was stuck in bad relationships. It was not until I was in my thirties that I learned the importance of discretion in regards to relationships with men. My heart had been bruised and broken many times, as men waltzed in and out of my life, and I'd never been the aggressor in the relationships, as they just seemed to appear in my life. I'd really given no thought to the actual characteristics of the type of man that I wanted to end up having as a marital partner. This is why I find it so amazing that I ended up with a wonderful husband, and I really do feel that he was hand selected just for me. By the time that I finally met him, thankfully, I had learned the lesson of discretion as to who to trust your heart to and whom not to.

Having found my life mate, I spoke to Alex about children and we considered adopting a child, but we decided that I would open up a business instead. Deep down inside, I'd always held a fear that I would have a child with a mental illness, and I didn't want to bring a troubled soul into this world. I had seen too many difficulties in regards to my mother's illness, to the extent that I worried that I carried a gene that would predispose my children to her disease. That combined with the actual fear of physical childbirth that my sister-in-law had shared with me helped to confirm that I would be childless. I sometimes regret the decision, I admit, as I love children and have missed out on the beautiful experience.

By the time I was in my late thirties, though, I had settled into being content as a business owner and was very happily married. Life was enjoyable and I had found the sense of peace that I'd been looking for. I didn't think that sense of contentment could be taken away so quickly and at a moment's notice. It was in August, two months after my fortieth birthday, that my life changed forever in losing my father. His stroke occurred without any warning and the shock of it left me stunned for months afterward, but dealing with the pain of loss and the aftermath in regards to my family relationships brought me many lessons. I learned how quickly life can be snatched away, and how important each moment spent with a loved one is, as it could be your last.

I also learned the importance of having the love and support of family and friends, even though tensions can sometimes run high. Caring so deeply can result in your heart feeling like it has split in two. I would rather be sensitive than have no feelings at all; losing someone so significant crushed me, but I know my father is close by and remains in my heart forever. Not having him in my life made me verify that I was so very much like him in so many ways. One discovery was, as you know, that my father had been the peacemaker in our family, and I didn't want to lose my family ties after he passed, so I tried hard to keep the family together.

It was not until my husband and I moved to Ohio five years later, when I was at the age of forty-five, that I walked away from feeling responsible for the outcome of family relationships. It was a slow progression, as I carried feelings of guilt about the physical move, but I was able to put the past behind me. I still participated in the care of my mother and kept in touch with everybody, but I mentally and physically walked away from their relationship issues. In my mind, I determined that they could work out their own problems and that I would simply do my best to remain on good terms with each one individually. I had finally decided that I was only responsible for myself and my own actions, and that they were responsible for theirs.

It was at this time that I finally stopped trying to be the mediator and healer of their relationships. I did continue to work on William for the next eighteen years, as I felt it was important for him to heal his relationship with our mother, keeping him abreast of her aging process and continually urging him to go visit with her.

At the time of this writing, I am in my late fifties and I am finally content to be the person that I have become. I feel like I have lived many lives, as it has taken me a long time to be comfortable in my own skin, but I have been through many of life's tutorials and I am positive I have many more to encounter. With a lot of hard work, I have healed from my past and forgiven not only myself, but those who hurt me in some way. Forgiveness is a way of healing, and I really do believe in the saying that "time does heals all wounds."

I am Kay

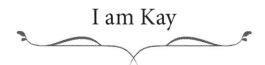

I am Kay. For most of my life, I have locked up who I really am inside of myself. Many times, I have been afraid to let myself go, fearing what other people may think. I can no longer hide from the world the person who I really am, though, and nor do I want to. I want my voice to be heard. For most of my life, I have walked along a narrow abyss that was filled with self-doubt and depression. I have worked hard to keep myself from falling permanently into that abyss, as I have had a taste of the water that flows there and do not wish to dive in. Keeping the light in and the darkness out is a work in progress, but worth the effort.

Being Kay has not been easy, as I have lived a life of interesting twists and turns along the road that I have traveled. The instruction book for my life was not very clear, and was difficult to figure out at times. Regardless, I decided a long time ago that I was going to be a person who *cared* about other people, and I was going to be kind to others – regardless of how others treated me. I have given this a lot of thought throughout my life, as one often ponders such things. In thinking about that choice, I have come to the conclusion that caring is exactly this, a choice. I don't think that you were born with a predisposition to care or not to care, as it is a decision that you have to make. In making the choice to be a person who cares, I have found the easier route at times would have been to just walk away. Walking away is not always easy, though, and a new set of problems will always find you if you try. Learning to have discretion about who to care about and who not to became my solution, as some situations became toxic to me and my health.

The lesson of discretion was a tough one, for who to give my love to and who was not worthy of my love was a challenging puzzle, as I always want to give my heart to everyone. I have found, though, that if you give love too easily, in most cases, it will be given to the wrong person and your good nature will end up being abused. If you don't think highly enough of yourself, you can believe me when I say that no one else will either. Having self-respect attracts the type of love you deserve because not everyone deserves a piece of the cake you have to offer. Some people will want the whole cake and there will be nothing left for you or anyone else.

I have given so much of myself to others at times that I had nothing left of my own energy to give. I know I have also been guilty of draining others of their time and energy, droning on about some injustice that was sent my way. In my heart, however, I know that the people who have touched my life have been there for a purpose. My greatest hope is that I have served that same purpose for someone else.

In November of 2015, I was on a search for my life purpose, as I was disheartened with a job that I held which wasn't meeting my expectations. I was disappointed with my position, as I realized that I no longer wanted to represent the organization. In my search for my life purpose, and for the answers that I was seeking, I walked into a mystic faire. It was at this faire that I met a wonderful astrologist and palm reader who encouraged me to tell my story. He somehow knew by looking at my palm that I had quite a story to share. During our conversation, he revealed that writing my story would be a healing process for me, and that it would also help someone else. In the past, I had started several times to write my story, and just could not get the words out, but he told me how it would work best for me, and that I could choose to follow his suggestion or not since we all have free will. I took the leap of faith and followed his instructions, and suddenly, I was easily able to put the pen to paper.

Strangely, the name of my book came about as a result of a mark the life path counselor saw on my hand. He noticed the blemish on my open palm and asked me how long it had been there. I had not noticed it before, and wondered what had made it appear. Maybe it had been there for a long time and I'd just never noticed it before. One day while sitting at my desk, though, I looked at the blemish, and the title of my book was born.

After that meeting, not only was the beginning of writing my story born, but I also seemed to find my voice. In January of 2016, I started to find my voice as I spoke out against some injustices that I'd come across in my employment. As a result of standing up for what I believed in, I lost my job, but it was a relief – as I had spent the last three years in a toxic environment. I looked at losing my job as a blessing, as it gave me the time to start working on my story; I was able to complete the rough draft prior to finding gainful employment. And at the time of this writing, I am working as a senior living consultant, marketing a program that helps seniors to stay in their own home for their long-term care needs.

If you are reading this book, I have no doubt that you chose it for a reason. Maybe you could identify with the title or something about the cover intrigued you enough for you to pick up the book. Whatever the reason, I hope that it has inspired you or helped you in some way, or maybe even encouraged you to tell your own story. We all have a story, after all, and your voice should be heard.

My story may be one that is unusual and strange in regards to my upbringing and the way that my life has evolved, but I have learned to embrace my uniqueness and I now love that about myself; I don't worry too much about what other people think. I have come to realize that I am the coin that does not fit into the candy machine, and I am alright with that. With all of the dents, bruises, scars, and tarnishes I have sustained, I've been able to keep the faith and hope that life is worth living. There is a power greater than me that has paved my path, and I am confident with the map that they are using. With a great big smile, I am happy to say that I am Kay, and I am blemished but not broken.

Printed in the United States
By Bookmasters